개정판

I'm Kitchen English

나는 키친잉글리시다

한선희 · 박미선 공저

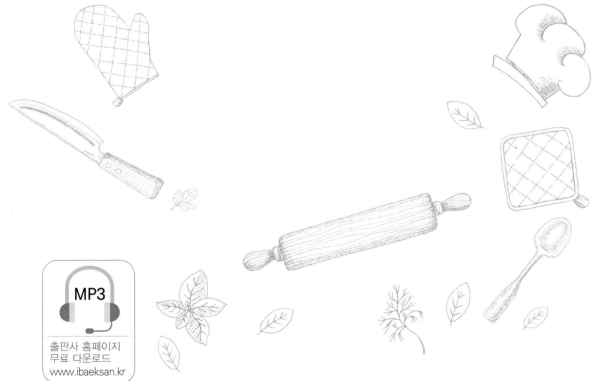

MP3
출판사 홈페이지
무료 다운로드
www.ibaeksan.kr

ⓑ (주)백산출판사

I'm Kitchen English(나는 키친 잉글리시다)

요리는 인간을 행복하게 한다고 합니다. 18~19세기에 "미각의 생리학"이란 저서로 프랑스 식탁 문화를 만들어낸 프랑스의 유명한 법관이자 미식가인 브리야 사바랭(1744~1826)은 "인간에게 새로운 요리를 발견하는 것은 새로운 별을 발견하는 것보다 인간을 더욱 행복하게 한다"(The discovery of a new dish does more for the happiness of mankind than the discovery of a star.)라는 유명한 말을 하였습니다. 저는 이 말을 영어 원문으로 읽고 '요리(dish)와 행복(happiness)'의 상관관계에 대해 생각해 보았습니다. 또한 어떤 이는 '행복'이라는 단어와 연관지어 제일 많이 떠오르는 단어는 '사랑하는 사람'과 '맛있는 음식'이라고 합니다. 요즘 요리 방송과 유명한 요리사들이 엄청난 인기를 끌고 있는데 이 현상 역시 '맛있는 음식'으로 행복을 추구하는 욕구로 인한 것이라 여겨집니다.

저(주저자 한선희)는 대학에서 영어를 꽤 오랜 세월 가르쳐 왔습니다. 영어영문학을 전공하여 영문학이나 언어학 등을 이론적으로 가르치던 학문적 시대를 거쳐, 영어과를 비롯하여 유아교육과, 항공서비스과 및 호텔외식서비스과 등 전공 직무별로 다양한 서비스 영어가 필요한 학과에서 학과 특성에 맞는 실용적인 영어를 가르치면서 영어교육 전공 저서들을 줄곧 집필해 왔습니다. 이를테면 토익, 영작문, 관광여행영어, 유아영어교육, 승무원영어, 레스토랑서비스영어 등의 저서들이었는데, 이 모든 것의 결정체가 바로 이번에 선보이는 키친 잉글리시 교재입니다. 저는 수년 전부터 키친 영어, 조리 영어를 가르쳐 오면서, 요리 전공자는 아닐지라도 요리와 행복의 상관관계를 아는 영어교육자로서 진정 행복하고 즐거운 기분으로 한 쪽 한 쪽 내용 구성에 노력을 기울였습니다. 전문 조리사를 꿈꾸는 학생들이 파란 눈의 외국인들과 함께 근무하는 키친에서 영어를 편안하고도 능숙하게 쓰는 모습을 상상하면서 행복감을 교재에서 미리 만끽했다고나 할까요.

"나는 키친 잉글리시다" 다소 건방져 보이기도 하는 이 책의 제목을 두고 꽤 오래 고심하였습니다만, 이미 "나는 레스토랑 영어다"라는 제목의 책을 얼마 전에 펴낸 적이 있기에 레스토랑 영어에서 키친 영어로 이어지는 연속 교재라는 차원에서 도전을 해보았습니다. "나는 키친 잉글리시다"라고 외치는 책 제목이 어필하는 효과가 분명히 있을 것입니다. 나도 충분히 할 수 있다고 마음 속에 숨겨둔 나만의 멘토가 나에게 키친 잉글리시에 대한 자신감을 가지라고 속삭이는 것 같지 않은가요? 우리 인간은 모두 가능성 넘치는 존재들입니다. 어느 누구든지 영어 기초가 없다고 지레 겁 먹지 말고, 자신에게 숨어있는 무궁무진한 가능성을 믿고 키친 잉글리시 공부에 도전해보면 좋겠습니다.

이 책의 공저자(박미선) 역시 학부에서 영어영문학을 전공하고, 언어학과 석사 및 영어교육학 박사를 취득한 영어교육 전문가로서, 한국 및 미국의 대학에서 다년간 강의하면서 한국 교육현장의 발음교육 및 실용영어교육에 대한 연구를 계속하고 있습니다. 이 교재에서 공저자는 각 단원의 음식, 키친, 조리 등에 관한 다양한 단어와 대화문들을 구성하는 것과 인터넷으로 무료 제공되는 ESL(English as a Second Language) 학습자들을 위한 유익한 레슨자료들을 정리하는 역할을 담당하였습니다.

이 책은 4개의 Chapter와 16개의 Unit으로 구성되어 있습니다. 전체적으로 보면, 주제별로 구성된 각 Unit마다 상황별 단어와 대화문 등을 통해 기본적인 영어 실력을 높이는 English Skill Up 파트와, 레시피를 읽고 쓰는 연습과 함께 조리 관련 지식 및 다양한 영문 레시피를 풍부하게 경험하게 함으로써 전반적인 키친 잉글리시 실력을 높이는 Culinary English 파트를 배치하였습니다.

구체적으로 보면, Chapter 1은 Kitchen과 Dining Room을 주제로 하였으며, Chapter 2는 음식 및 식사를 주제로 삼아 5개의 Unit을 구성하였습니다. Chapter 3에서는 본격적인 조리 영어에 돌입하여 샐러드, 수프, 빵, 해산물 요리, 로스팅, 브로일링 등으로 6개의 Unit을 구성하였으며, 마지막 Chapter 4에서는 감자, 초콜릿, 겨자 등 유명 음식들을 주제로 한 가벼운 리딩으로 3개의 Unit을 구성하였습니다. 교재와 함께 원어민들의 녹음 자료도 수업 중에 효과적으로 활용할 수 있습니다. 단어와 대화문 따라 읽기를 통해 말하기, 듣기, 읽기, 쓰기의 네 가지 목표를 모두 달성할 수 있도록 하였습니다.

어느 분야에서도 마찬가지겠지만 특히 글로벌 시대의 조리 외식 분야에서도 영어 실력 없이는 진정한 전문인이 될 수 없습니다. 유창한 영어 실력으로 자신의 직업에서 더욱 행복감을 느낄 수 있는 자신 있는 전문인으로 성장하기 위한 과정에 이 책이 도움이 되기를 바라며, 교실이나 학교 조리실에서뿐 아니라 집안 부엌에서도 최고급 호텔 레스토랑의 주방에서도 살아서 움직이는 책이 되기를 소망합니다.

마지막으로 초판 출판에 이어 개정판 출판까지 흔쾌히 허락해주신 (주)백산출판사에 진심으로 감사를 드립니다.

2019년 7월
관악산 기슭에서

Chapter 1 **Kitchen & Dining Room**

Unit·1 The Kitchen | 8

Unit·2 The Dining Room | 21

Chapter 2 **Food**

Unit·3 Fruit | 32

Unit·4 Vegetables | 43

Unit·5 Meat, Seafood & Poultry | 56

Unit·6 Breakfast, Lunch & Dinner | 71

Unit·7 Dessert, Fast Food & Junk Food | 94

Chapter 3 **Cuisine English**

Unit·8 Salads | 116

Unit·9 Soups | 129

Unit·10 Seafood | 147

Unit·11 Bread | 158

Unit·12 Roasting | 175

Unit·13 Broiling | 196

Chapter 4 **Story of Food**

Unit·14 Potatoes | 210

Unit·15 Chocolate | 225

Unit·16 Mustard | 235

부록: 조리용어 | 248

1

Kitchen & Dining Room

Unit·1 The Kitchen
Unit·2 The Dining Room

학습목표

1. 키친 잉글리시를 사용하는 직접 현장인 Kitchen과 Dining Room을 중심으로 관련된 기본단어와 회화표현들을 익혀 활용할 수 있게 한다.

2. Culinary 영어의 기본이 되는 레시피를 작성하는 영어 기본문형 및 문법을 학습하고 쉬운 레시피를 읽고 이해할 수 있게 한다.

UNIT 1 The Kitchen

Part 1 · English Skill Up

1. Vocabulary Preview
2. Classroom Activities
3. Dialogues
4. English for Fun

Part 2 · Culinary English

1. Brillat Savarin(브리야 샤바랭)
2. Organization of the Kitchen(주방 조직도)
3. Writing Recipes(레시피 작성의 기본연습)
4. Cuisine Quiz(조리 퀴즈)

Part 1 — English Skill Up

1. Vocabulary Preview 🎧

burner	
cabinet	
can opener	
coffee maker	
creamer	
cupboard	
dishpan	dishwasher
dryer	electric mixer
faucet	freezer
frying pan	linoleum
oven	pot
refrigerator	sink
small appliance	stove
sugar bowl	tea kettle
toaster	washing machine
wok	

✏️ **Words to Note**

cupboard	faucet	tea kettle	wok
[kấbɔːrd]	[fɔːsɪt]	차 주전자	(금속제의)
찬장, 벽장	(물통·수도 따위의) 물 꼭지, 물주둥이, 마개		중국 요리 냄비

2. Classroom Activities

What's the story?

- Work in groups of five.

- Write a story about the kitchen.

- Everyone in the group should contribute at least two sentences.

- Read your story to the class.

3. Dialogues 🎧

Dialogue 1

A Your kitchen is so different from mine, Maria!

B Well, there are some things that are the same.

A Yes, we both have a refrigerator, a stove, and a sink. But you have a microwave... and a dishwasher.

B I know. I love modern conveniences. I just bought an electric rice cooker!

A Where will you put it? You don't have much counter space.

B I'll find the space. I make rice every day.

A You're a good cook, Maria. I remember that wonderful vegetarian dinner you cooked for me.

B Well, you make a great sandwich!

A That's about all I can make in my tiny kitchen. I eat out a lot. Hey, do you want to grab a bite to eat now?

Notes

convenience 편리함

vegetarian 채식주의자

grab 움켜잡다, (게걸스럽게) 먹다

electric rice cooker 전기밥솥

tiny 작은

Dialogue 2

A What's your favorite room in your house, Erin?

B **Definitely** the kitchen.

A Really? Why?

B When I was a child, the kitchen was the center of my family's life.

A I remember that my mother was always busy in the kitchen.

B Mine, too. And we all did our homework at the kitchen table.

A So did we. It was great to be near the snacks!

B My mother always **kept an eye on** us so we wouldn't **fool around**!

Notes

definitely 결정적으로

fool around 바보짓 하며 다니다

keep an eye on ~ ~를 주시하다

Parts of the Kitchen

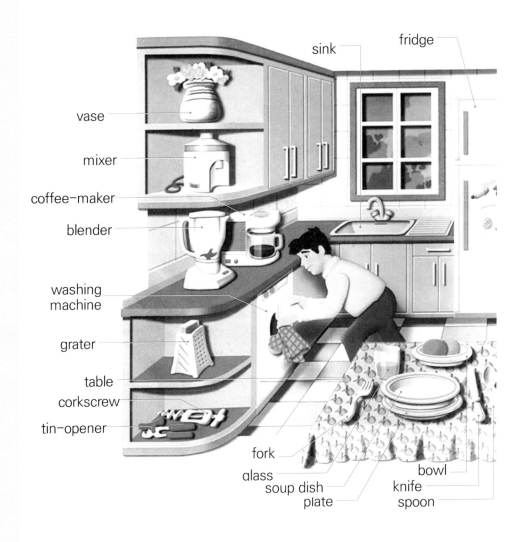

vase

mixer

coffee-maker

blender

washing
machine

grater

table

corkscrew

tin-opener

sink

fridge

fork

glass

soup dish

plate

bowl

knife

spoon

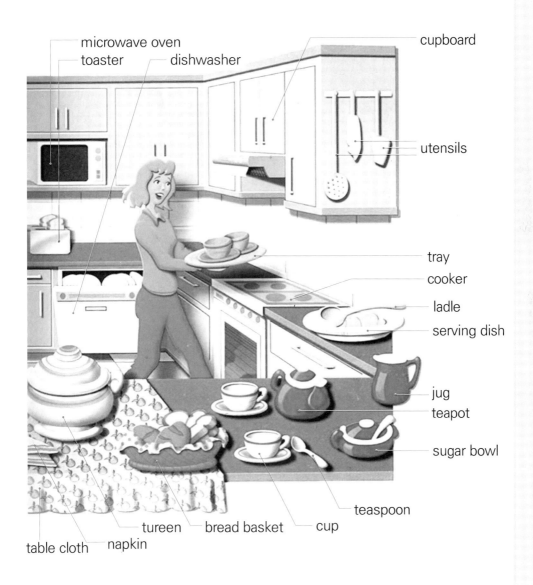

microwave oven

toaster dishwasher

cupboard

utensils

tray

cooker

ladle

serving dish

jug

teapot

sugar bowl

teaspoon

tureen bread basket cup

table cloth napkin

출처 https://www.easypacelearning.com/all-lessons/learning-english-level-
1/1179-kitchen-vocabulary-english-words-and-pictures

4. English for Fun

Kitchen의 어원

부엌(Kitchen)은 영어 고어인 'Cycene'과 '요리하다'라는 뜻의 라틴어 '코쿠에레(Coquere)'에서 유래되었다. 속어로 오케스트라의 타악기 파트를 이르는 말이다. 비슷한 뜻의 단어들은 다음과 같다.

cuisine 요리, 요리법, 주방, 조리실

culinary 주방의, 요리의, 요리에 쓰는

The Culinary Institute of America, CIA

(더 컬리너리 인스티튜트 오브 아메리카) 요리계의 하버드 대학교, 미국조리사관학교라 불리는 미국 최고의 명문 요리 학교, CIA는 독립적인 비영리 전문 대학이며, 세계 최고 수준의 전문 요리 교양과 기술 교육을 제공한다. (위키백과)

Part 2 — Culinary English

1. Brillat Savarin (브리야 샤바랭)

1755년 4월 1일 ~ 1826년 2월 2일 프랑스 파리 출생.

"그대 무엇을 먹는지 말하라, 그러면 나는 그대가 누군지 말해보겠다."

(Tell me what you eat, and I will tell you what you are.)

이 유명한 말을 한 브리야 샤바랭은 프랑스의 법관이자 미식가로, 프랑스와 미국의 사법계에서 법관으로 활동했으나 미식평론가로서 더 명성을 얻었다. 그의 저서 〈미식예찬〉(원제는 '미각의 생리학', Physiologie du goût)은 그의 대표적 저서이다. 이 책은 맛의 생리학 및 식도락에 관한 유명한 책이다. 요리법에 대한 연구서라기보다는 식사 중에 즐거움을 더해 줄 수 있는 온갖 종류의 한담과 교훈, 일화, 관찰들을 재치있게 모아놓은 것으로 요리법은 간간이 실려 있을 뿐이다. 이 책은 19세기에 여러 차례 중판되었으며 1925년 영어로 번역되었다.

브리야 샤바랭의 어록(Wikipeida Quotes)

1. Tell me what you eat, and I will tell you what you are.

   그대 무엇을 먹는지 말하라, 그러면 나는 그대가 누군지 말해보겠다.

2. An avid cheese lover, Brillat-Savarin remarked: "A dessert without cheese is like a beautiful woman with only one eye."

   열렬한 치즈 애호가인 브리야 샤바랭은 이렇게 말했다, "치즈가 없는 디저트는 눈 하나만 있는 예쁜 여성과 같다."

3. To invite someone is to take charge of his happiness, the whole time he is under our roof.

   누군가를 초대한다는 것은 그가 우리 집 지붕아래 있는 모든 시간 동안 그의 행복을 책임지는 것이다.

4. Someone who receives his friends without giving any personal attention to the meal prepared for them is not worthy of having friends.

   친구를 위해 어떤 음식을 준비할 것인가에 대한 개별적인 관심도 없이 친구를 맞이하는 사람은 친구를 얻을 가치도 없는 사람이다.

5. The discovery of a new dish does more for the happiness of mankind than the discovery of a star.

   새로운 요리를 발견하는 것은 인류의 행복을 위해서 새로운 행성을 발견하는 것 이상이다.

2. Organization of The Kitchen (주방 조직도)

Executive Chef
이그제큐티브 셰프, 총주방장
Executive Sous Chef
이그제큐티브 수 셰프, 부총주방장
Chef
셰프, 주방장
Section Chef
부서 주방장
Head Cook
수석 조리장
1st Cook
1급 조리장
2nd Cook
2급 조리장
3rd Cook
3급 조리장

기타 Cook Helper = Apprentice 보조조리사, Trainee 조리실습생

3. Writing Recipes (레시피 작성의 기본연습)

When you write instructions in your recipes, you must use exact words to describe each step. It is also important to give all the steps in the correct order. Look at these pictures. Put them in the correct order. Then fill in the blanks with the words below the pictures.

fill   put   pour   leave   boil

_____ for a few minutes.

_____ the tea into the cup.

_____ some tea into the teapot.

__Fill__ the kettle with water.

_____ the water.

_____ the teapot with boiling water.

for a few minutes.

some tea into the teapot.

the water.

the tea into the cup.

(1) Fill   the kettle with water.

the teapot with boiling water.

Exercise
Now write the complete sentence in the correct order.

1.

2.

3.

4.

5.

6.

Grammar for English Recipe Reading Comprehension

레시피의 기본 문장 : 명령문(동사로 시작한다)

동사 (-하라)	목적어 (-를)	부사 혹은 부사구(전치사＋명사), 부사절(조건, 때) (-에다가, - 할 때에)

Make a full sentence using the words given in the bracket.

1. 차 주전자에 물을 채우세요.(the water, the tea kettle, with, fill)

2. 브로콜리를 끓는 물에 살짝 데치세요.(the boiling water, the broccoli, blanch, in, lightly)

3. 배추를 4등분 하세요.(the cabbage, into, cut, 4 pieces)

4. Cuisine Quiz (조리 퀴즈)

Quiz about Bread

1. The principal gas formed by growing Yeast is   .

2. In a chiffon cake, what is used in the recipe instead of fat?

The Dining Room

Part 1 · English Skill Up

1. Vocabulary Preview
2. Classroom Activities
3. Dialogues
4. English for Fun

Part 2 · Culinary English

1. Recipe Reading & Writing Exercise(레시피 연습)
2. Table d'hote setting(정식 상차림)
3. My Favorite Recipe(내가 좋아하는 레시피)
4. Cuisine Quiz(조리 퀴즈)

Part 1 — English Skill Up

1. Vocabulary Preview 🎧

candlestick	
glass	
napkin	
pepper shaker	
pie server	
pitcher	
plate	salad bowl
salt shaker	saucer
serving spoon	set the table
silverware	soup bowl
table cloth	table spoon
teaspoon	vase
main course fork	main course knife
first course fork	first course knife
side plate	dessert spoon and fork

✎ *Words to Note*

silverware
은식기류

saucer
(커피 잔 따위의) 받침
접시 모양의 물건

2. Classroom Activities

Partner Interview

Partner's Name: _____

*Practice these questions with your partner.

Q1. What room do you eat in at home?

Q2. How do you set the table at home? for breakfast? lunch? dinner?

Q3. Does your family always eat together?

Group Activity

- Work in groups of four or five.

- With your group, list five things people say at the dinner table.

- Read your list to the class.

- Make a list on the board.

3. Dialogues 🎧

Dialogue 1

A Do you have a dining room in your house?

B Are you kidding? I have a small apartment!

A I **meant**, did you have a dining room when you were a child?

B No, we didn't. Did you?

A Yes. We ate dinner there every night.

B What was it like?

A It was pretty **formal**. It had a glass table and eight chairs. My mom taught us how to set the table. First, we always put a white tablecloth on the table. Then we put the plates, **silverware**, glasses, and napkins on the table.

B Sounds pretty formal. We ate in the kitchen at a large, round table.

A I bet you had more fun!

Notes   meant mean의 과거형   formal 격식을 갖춘 (반대말 informal)
silverware 은식기류

4. English for Fun

1) Reading: Healthy Family Meals 🎧

The Shin family is trying to eat healthy meals, but it is difficult. Both Mr. and Mrs. Shin work all day, and they are tired when they get home.

They also have two young sons who need a lot of attention. Their oldest son is seven years old and the younger son is nine months old. It is difficult for the Shins to plan healthy family meals when they have such a busy schedule. Lately, the family has been eating fast food that Mr. Shin picks up on the way home from  work. This is a bad habit, and the Shins are worried that their children will develop poor eating habits. They want to start eating healthy homemade meals.

2) True of False

1.   Mr. and Mrs. Shin are married, and they have three children.

2.   Eating fast food for dinner is a bad habit.

3.   Mrs. Shin is tired when she gets home from work.

4.   The baby in the picture is sitting in a high chair and drinking a bottle.

5.   It is difficult to plan healthy family meals because the Shins are busy.

Part 2 — Culinary English

1. Recipe Reading & Writing Exercise (레시피 연습)

자주 나오는 동사 연습

mince 다지다	peel 껍질을 벗기다	boil 끓이다
mash 짓이기다	chop 잘게 다지다	fry 튀기다
stir 젓다	add 더하다	bake 굽다

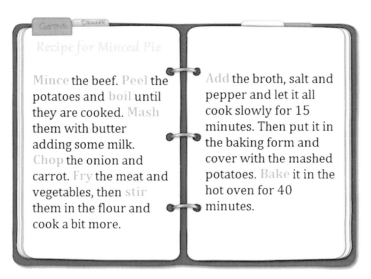

Recipe for Minced Pie

Mince the beef. Peel the potatoes and boil until they are cooked. Mash them with butter adding some milk. Chop the onion and carrot. Fry the meat and vegetables, then stir them in the flour and cook a bit more.

Add the broth, salt and pepper and let it all cook slowly for 15 minutes. Then put it in the baking form and cover with the mashed potatoes. Bake it in the hot oven for 40 minutes.

출처_ islcollective.com

* Read the recipe for minced pie and study the verbs that follow.

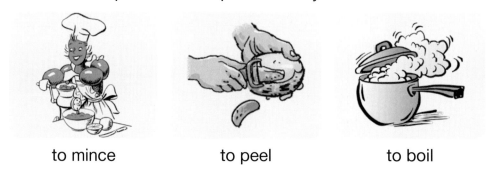

to mince	to peel	to boil

to mash | to chop | to fry

to stir | to add | to bake

2. Table d'hote setting (정식 상차림)

❶ Show Plate : 쇼 플레이트, 일종의 장식용 접시, 시각적 효과를 주고 테이블 세팅 시 균형을 잡아준다.

❷ Napkin : 처음에는 냅킨을 접힌 채 누워있는 상태로 놓는다. 테이블 세팅이 다

끝난 다음 이상이 없으면 냅킨을 세움

❸ Appetizer Knife : 애피타이저 나이프

❹ Soup Spoon : 수프 스푼

❺ Fish Knife : 생선용 나이프

❻ Meat(Dinner) Knife : 육류용(디너) 나이프

❼ Appetizer Fork : 애피타이저 포크

❽ Fish Fork : 생선용 포크

❾ Salad Fork : 샐러드 포크

❿ Meat(Dinner) Fork : 육류용(디너) 포크

⓫ Dessert Spoon : 디저트 스푼, 디저트 포크와 함께 쇼 플레이트 위쪽에 위치

⓬ Dessert Fork : 디저트 포크

⓭ Butter Knife : 버터 나이프

⓮ B&B Plate : 쇼 플레이트 왼쪽에 놓는다. 빵(bread)과 버터(butter)를 놓는 접시를 말함

⓯ Butter Bowl : 버터 볼

⓰ Water Goblet : 물잔

⓱ White Wine Glass : 백포도주 잔

⓲ Red Wine Glass : 적포도주 잔

⓳ Champagne Glass : 샴페인 잔

⓴ Salt & Pepper(Caster Set) : 소금 & 후추

3. My Favorite Recipe (내가 좋아하는 레시피)

· Fruitcake

When is your parents' **wedding anniversary**? Do you want to bake a special cake for them? I, an able chef, **recommend** this recipe for fruitcake. This is My Favorite Recipe for

fruitcake. This is rather a traditional recipe for fruitcake, but everybody says it's **fantastic**!

Directions

1. Put 3 cups of flour into a mixing bowl.

2. Add a little sugar.

3. Slice a few oranges.

4. Cut up a few oranges.

5. Pour in a little honey.

6. Add a little baking soda.

7. Chop up a few nuts.

8. Add a little salt.

9. Mix in a few raisins.

10. Bake for 45 minutes.

Notes	wedding anniversary 결혼기념일	recommend 추천하다
	fantastic 환상적인	slice 얇게 썰다
	cut up, chop up ~을 잘게 썰다	pour in ~을 붓다
	raisin 건포도	

4. Cuisine Quiz (조리 퀴즈)

1. You should carry hot containers with which kind of towels?

    a. Wet   b. Dry

2. If you drop a knife,

    a. Step back and do not try to catch it.

    b. Grab the handle before it drops too far.

    c. Try to kick it away from your legs.

CHAPTER

2

Food

Unit·3 Fruit

Unit·4 Vegetables

Unit·5 Meat, Seafood & Poultry

Unit·6 Breakfast, Lunch & Dinner

Unit·7 Dessert, Fast Food & Junk Food

학습목표

1. 요리에 사용되는 재료를 영어로 표현할 수 있다. 과일, 채소, 고기, 해산물, 가금류, 양념 등의 영어단어를 익혀 영문 레시피 이해가 쉽도록 한다.

2. 과일, 야채 등의 식재료와, 아침, 점심, 저녁 및 디저트와 패스트푸드 등의 기본 메뉴에 대한 영어표현을 할 수 있게 한다.

UNIT 3 Fruit

Part 1 · English Skill Up

1. Vocabulary Preview
2. Classroom Activities
3. Dialogues
4. English for Fun

Part 2 · Culinary English

1. Recipe Reading & Writing Exercise(레시피 연습)
2. My Favorite Recipe(내가 좋아하는 레시피)
3. Cuisine Quiz(조리 퀴즈)

Part 1 — English Skill Up

1. Vocabulary Preview 🎧

almond	
apple	
apricot	
avocado	
banana	
blackberry	
blueberry	cantaloupe
cherry	chestnut
coconut	jujube
grape	grapefruit
kiwi	lemon
lime	mandarine
mango	orange
papaya	peach
peanut	pear
persimmon	pineapple
plum	prune
raspberry	strawberry
tomato	walnut
watermelon	box
bunch	buy
pit	pound
seed	skin

cantaloupe	plum	lime	mandarin
멜론의 일종	자두	라임	귤, 감귤
	prune		
	말린 자두		

2. Classroom Activities

Partner Interview

Partner's Name: _____

* Practice these questions with your partner.

Q1. What is your favorite kind of fruit?

Q2. What other fruit do you like?

Group Game: "Preparing Fruit Salad"

- Work in groups of four. Prepare a fruit salad for the next class.

- To Get Ready:

★ What kind of fruit will each student bring?

Who will bring a bowl?

Who will bring a knife?

Who will bring a large spoon?

Who will bring a fork?

To Demonstrate:

1. Prepare your fruit salad.

2. Compare the fruit salads.

3. Vote on the best one.

4. Enjoy the snack.

3. Dialogues 🎧

Dialogue 1

A What's your favorite fruit, Jeff?

B Oh, I love all kinds of fruit, Gail.

A Me, too. But what do you like best?

B Well, I think maybe oranges.

A Mmm. I like oranges, too. What other fruits do you like?

B Grapefruit. I love grapefruit. And cherries – but I don't like the pits.

A How about grapes and watermelon?

B Yes, but not the seeds. I like seedless grapes and seedless watermelon better. Boy, this conversation is making me hungry for some fruit!

A Me, too!

Notes pit (배, 복숭아 등의) 씨   seed 씨
seedless 씨 없는

Dialogue 2

A Hey, let's make a fruit salad!

B,C,D Great idea! Sounds good! Yeah!

B OK. We can each bring something for the salad.

C I'll bring a bowl and a large spoon.

D I'll bring a knife — I have a sharp knife.

B I'll bring plates and forks.

A What about the fruit? My favorites are oranges and grapefruits.

D Mmm-hmm! And I love melons — watermelons and cantaloupes!

C Don't forget grapes and bananas and apples.

B Bring everything tomorrow, and we'll make the fruit salad for lunch.

A,C,D Yum! Sounds great! All right!

4. English for Fun

• Grammar Rap

1) Where's Charlie?

Where's Charlie?

    He's in the kitchen.

What's he doing?

    Eating lunch.

Charlie's in the kitchen eating lunch.

    Charlie's in the kitchen eating lunch.

Who's in the kitchen?

    Charlie's in the kitchen.

What's he doing?

    Eating lunch.

Where's Betty?

    She's in the dining room.

What's she doing?

    Eating an apple.

Betty's in the dining room eating an apple.

    Betty's in the dining room eating an apple.

Who's in the dining room?

    Betty's in the dining room.

What's she doing?

    Eating an apple.

2) I Smile When I'm Happy.

I smile when I'm happy.

　　I frown when I'm sad.

I blush when I'm embarrassed.

　　And I shout when I'm mad.

Are you smiling?

　　Yes. I'm happy

Are you frowning?

　　Yes. I'm sad.

Are you blushing?

　　I'm embarrassed.

Are you shouting?

　　Yes, I'm mad.

We smile when we're happy.

　　We frown when we're sad.

We blush when we're embarrassed.

　　And we shout when we're mad.

We smile when we're happy.

　　We frown when we're sad.

We blush when we're embarrassed.

　　And we shout when we're mad.

Part 2 — Culinary English

1. Recipe Reading & Writing Exercise (레시피 연습)

• Lemon Yogurt Cake

* Read the recipe and match the instructions with the pictures.

Directions

1. Preheat the oven to 180℃

2. Crack the three eggs into a bowl. Mix with an electric mixer.

3. Add the sugar and the plain yogurt. Mix again with the electric mixer.

4. Add the rest of the ingredients, flour, oil, pinch of salt, baking powder and grated lemon peel. Mix again.

5. Pour it into a baking pan.

6. Put it inside the oven.

7. Bake it for 45 minutes. Don't open the oven while baking.

* Underline all of the verbs in the recipe.

2. My Favorite Recipe (내가 좋아하는 레시피)

• Vegetable Stew

Do you want to **hold a party** soon? Are you going to cook **something special** for someone? As a famous chef, I recommend this recipe for vegetable stew. This is My Favorite Recipe for vegetable stew. It is really easy to make and delicious, so everybody says it's **marvelous** and they love it!

Directions

1. Put a little butter into a **saucepan**.
2. Chop up a few onions.
3. Cut up a few potatoes.
4. Pour in a little wine.
5. Slice a few carrots
6. Add a little salt.
7. Chop up a few mushrooms.
8. Slice a little tomatoes.
9. Add a little pepper
10. Cook for 3 hours.

| hold a party 파티를 열다 | something special 특별한 것 |
| marvelous 놀라운 | saucepan 냄비 |

3. Cuisine Quiz (조리 퀴즈)

1. Another source of steam is a kettle on a stove.
When lifting its cover,   .

  a. Remove the cover quickly.
  b. Lift the edge toward you first.
  c. Lift the edge away from you first

2. When a kettle is steaming, its contents are hot. To avoid burns,
you should use a long handled tool for stirring.

  a. True   b. False

UNIT 4 Vegetables

Part 1 · English Skill Up

1. Vocabulary Preview
2. Classroom Activities
3. Dialogues
4. English for Fun

Part 2 · Culinary English

1. Recipe Reading & Writing Exercise(레시피 연습)
2. My Favorite Recipe(내가 좋아하는 레시피)
3. Cuisine Quiz(조리 퀴즈)

Part 1 — English Skill Up

1. Vocabulary Preview 🎧

artichoke	
asparagus	
bamboo-root	
bean	
bean-sprout	
beet	
broccoli	cabbage
carrot	cauliflower
celery	Chili-pepper
cinnamon	corn
cucumber	eggplant
garlic	ginger
ginseng	Korean-cabbage
lettuce	mint
mushroom	mustard
onion	paprika
parsley	peas
pepper	potato
pumpkin	sesame-leaf
spinach	tomato
zucchini	ear
bunch	fresh
head	produce

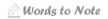

cauliflower
꽃양배추

zucchini
[zukːni]
애호박, 서양호박

artichoke
아티초크

2. Classroom Activities

Partner Interview

Partner's Name: _____

* Practice these questions with your partner.

Q1. What is your favorite vegetable?

Q2. What vegetables don't you like?

Q3. What vegetables do you usually use for salad?

Q4. Which vegetables do you buy by the bunch? by the head? by the ear? by the pound?

Group Decision: "Vegetable Salad"

* Work in groups of five or six.

1. Decide which vegetables to use for a salad.

2. Decide how to prepare each vegetable.

VEGETABLE	YES/NO	COOKED	RAW	PEELED	SLICED	SHREDDED
other						
TOTALS						

To Demonstrate:

Tell the class about your salad

3. Dialogues 🎧

Dialogue 1

A Hi. Can I help you?

B Yes. What vegetables are good today?

A Let's see... everything is good, but the corn and the cabbage are especially fresh.

B That corn does look good! I'll take a half dozen ears, please.

A Yes, the corn is a good buy. It's in season. Anything else?

B The tomatoes look great. I'll take four. And a head of lettuce.

A How about some beans? They just came in this morning.

B OK. A pound of beans. That's all for today. By the way, what's your dog's name?

A Veggie. He loves all kinds of vegetables. Here, Veggie, want a carrot?

B Woof! Woof!

a half dozen 반 다스
ear (옥수수 등) 헤아리는 단위(ex: an ear of corn)
in season 제철의
head (양배추 등) 헤아리는 단위(ex: a head of cabbage)
woof 낮게 으르렁거리다

Dialogue 2

A We'd like to show you our salad. This is how we made it. We each brought in a different vegetable and prepared it together.

B I brought in a head of lettuce.

C Carol and I washed the lettuce. Then I **shredded** it and put it in the bowl.

D I brought in a bunch of carrots. I peeled them and cut them up.

C I cooked the beets and sliced them at home.

A I don't like vegetables, but I brought in some mushr ooms, anyway.

D We mixed all the vegetables together, and then we added salad dressing.

B And here it is! We hope you enjoy it!

Notes shred 길게 쪼개다

Dialogue 3 (Pattern Drill)

Customer 1   How much does **a head of lettuce** cost?

Clerk 1   Ninety-five cents.

Customer 1   Ninety-five cents? That's a lot of money!

Clerk 1   You're right. Lettuce is very expensive this week.

~ ~ ~ ~

Customer 2   How much does **a pound of apples** cost?

Clerk 2   A dollar twenty-five.

Customer 2   A dollar twenty-five? That's a lot of money!

Clerk 2   You're right! Apples are very expensive this week.

Notes a head of lettuce 양상추 1통   a pound of apples 사과 1파운드

4. English for Fun

* Match the following.

1. a loaf of   •   • oranges

2. a pound of   •   • eggs

3. a pound of   •   • soda

4. a bunch of   •   • bread

5. a quart of   •   • carrots

6. a bottle of   •   • milk

7. a few pounds of •   • Swiss cheese

8. a bag of   •   • onions

9. a dozen   •   • butter

Part 2 — Culinary English

1. Recipe Reading & Writing Exercise (레시피 연습)

Common English Verbs in Recipes(레시피에 자주 등장하는 동사)

영문 레시피에서 가장 빈도수가 높은 동사는 다음과 같다.

Peel	Remove the outer covering from a fruit, vegetable.	(과일, 야채의) 껍질을 벗기다
Slice	Cut a thicker piece of food into slices.	얇게 자르다
Grate	Rub food against a grater so is cut it into a lot of small pieces.	식품을 문질러 갈다, 치즈 등을 갈다
Pour	Pour the milk, water into the bowl	우유, 물 등을 붓다
Mix	Combine food / liquid together so it becomes one.	식품을 혼합하다
Whisk	A utensil needed for whipping eggs or cream very quickly	계란, 크림 등을 빨리 젓다, 혹은 젓는 도구
Boil	Heat liquid until it boils.	끓이다, 삶다
Fry	Cook food in very hot oil.	뜨거운 기름으로 튀기다
Roll	A Rolling pin is used for making pastry flat and making cake shapes.	굴리다, 반죽을 평평하게 하고 케이크 모양을 만드는데 롤링 핀(홍두깨)을 사용
Stir	Move a spoon around in a pan in a circle	숟가락으로 팬 속을 이리저리 휘젓다
Simmer	Heat liquid or food below the boiling point and let it bubble gently	끓는점 아래로 액체나 음식을 서서히 부글부글 끓이다, 약한 불에 오랫동안 끓이다

Poach	Cook eggs or fish in or over boiling water.	끓는 물 속에서 계란을 익히다. 생선 또한 Poaching을 하다.
Bake	Cook food without a flame, in an oven.	불꽃 없이 오븐 속에서 굽다
Roast	Cook meat a long time in an oven or over a fire	오븐에서 오래 굽다
Grill/ BBQ	Cook food under heat from a metal bar or flame.	석쇠 구이하다, 바비큐하다
Melt	Make liquefied by using a form of heat	열 형태를 이용하여 액체화시키다, 녹이다
Spread	Spread butter or jam onto bread	(빵에 잼을) 바르다, (버터를) 바르다(버터, 소스 등을) 펴 바르다
Taste	to eat or drink a little of.	맛보다

Check for Common Recipe Verbs:

아래 각각의 그림에 해당하는 영어 동사를 위 표에서 찾아서 영어로 적어보세요.

English Imperative (영어의 명령법)

In English, recipes largely contain verbs conjugated into the imperative mood. Examples of verbs in the imperative mood include the following: (영어 레시피에는 명령법으로 동사가 맨 먼저 나온다.)

Boil the potatoes. (감자를 삶으세요)

Dice the vegetables. (야채를 깍둑썰기 하세요)

Do not overcook the pasta. (파스타를 지나치게 익히지 마세요)

Do not melt the butter. (버터를 녹이지 마세요)

레시피의 기본 문장: 명령문 (동사로 시작한다)

동사 (-하라)	목적어 (-를)	부사 혹은 부사구(전치사＋명사), 부사절(조건, 때) (-에다가, – 할 때에)

Make a full sentence using the words given in the bracket.

1. 팬에 기름을 달구어라.(in pan, the oil, heat)

2. 식초와 오일을 항아리 속에 넣어라.(the vinegar, place, in a jar, and oil)

3. 고기가 부드러워질 때까지 천천히 요리하라.(the meat, tender, simmer, until)

4. 양파를 가늘게 썰어라.(thinly, slice, the onions)

2. My Favorite Recipe (내가 좋아하는 레시피)

• Mashed Potatoes (serves 4~6 persons)

Ingredients

1.2kg	high-starch potatoes
90g	unsalted butter, at room temperature
120ml	whole milk
1 tsp	salt
pinch	freshly ground black pepper or white pepper

Directions

1. Scrub and rinse the potatoes.

2. Cook the potatoes in a boiling water.

3. Peel the potatoes.

4. Mash the potatoes with the masher.

5. Add milk and butter and combine them well with a spoon.

6. **Adjust** the **seasoning** with salt and pepper.

> **Notes**
>
> | | |
> |---|---|
> | ingredient 식재료 | high-starch 고녹말 |
> | whole milk 전유(유지방을 제거하지 않은 생우유) | pinch 약간 |
> | ground 갈은(grind 갈다) | scrub 문지르다 |
> | peel 껍질을 벗기다(peeler 껍질을 벗기는 기기) | seasoning 양념 |
> | masher 감자 으깨는 도구(mash 으깨다) | adjust 조절하다 |

3. Cuisine Quiz (조리 퀴즈)

1. One of the most common methods of cooking vegetable is boiling. Which of the following is the most serious problem when boiling vegetables?

a. The danger of overcooking
b. The danger of undercooking

2. The red color of beets and red cabbage can be maintained by adding a small amount of vinegar.

a. True   b. False

UNIT 5 Meat, Seafood & Poultry

Part 1 · English Skill Up

1. Vocabulary Preview
2. Classroom Activities
3. Dialogues
4. English for Fun

Part 2 · Culinary English

1. Recipe Reading & Writing Exercise(레시피 연습)
2. About Eggs(계란)
3. My Favorite Recipe(내가 좋아하는 레시피)
4. Cuisine Quiz(조리 퀴즈)

Part 1 — English Skill Up

1. Vocabulary Preview 🎧

can	
chicken	
crab	
meat	
fish	
ground-beef	
ham	hot-dogs
lamb-chops	lamb-roast
leg-of-lamb	liver
lobster	meatballs
octopus	pig's-feet
pork-chops	roast-beef
sausages	shellfish
shrimp	steak
stew-beef	swordfish
tuna	tuna-fish
package	

Words to Note

octopus
문어

swordfish
황새치, 갈치

2. Classroom Activities

Partner Interview

* Practice these questions with your teacher and partner.

Q1. Do you eat meat? What is your favorite meat?

Q2. Do you eat poultry? What is your favorite?

Q3. Do you eat fish? What is your favorite fish? What is your favorite shellfish?

Q4. Are there any meats, fish, and poultry that you never eat? Why?

Q5. Where do you buy meats? fish? poultry?

Q6. Is it a good idea to eat a lot of red meat? Why? Why not?

3. Dialogues 🎧

Dialogue 1

A I'm glad you're coming for dinner tonight, Paco. Do you eat **poultry**?

B Do you mean chicken?

A Yes, chicken or turkey. Which do you prefer? Or would you prefer red meat?

B Well, Maria, I don't really eat red meat.

A I don't eat much red meat, either. How about some seafood? Fish? **Shrimp**?

B Well... I don't really care too much for fish, either, Maria.

A That's OK. How about pork chops, then?

B **Actually**, Maria, I'm a **vegetarian**. I don't usually eat any meat at all. But I know I'll like anything you cook!

Notes		
poultry 가금류		shrimp 새우
actually 사실상		vegetarian 채식주의자

Dialogue 2

A Karen, do you understand this Find Someone Who?

B I think so.

A We need to find classmates who like food a certain way, right?

B Yes. Let's start with you, Don. Do you like baked fish with salt and pepper?

A Well, I like salt and pepper, but I don't like baked fish!

B OK. Now I'll ask Steve. Oh, Steve, do you like baked fish with salt and pepper?

C Yes, I love it! Now, let me ask you and Don Question Two. Do you like barbecued spare ribs?

B What's that?

C I'm not sure! Do you know what they are, Don?

A Yeah, I think they're... umm... Let's ask the teacher.

Notes	rib 갈비	spare ribs 돼지갈비구이

4. English for Fun

• Grammar Tips: Measuring Words

1) Dialogue: A Shopping List 🎧

Listen and fill in the blanks.

Jay   What are you writing, Dad?

Father   A shopping list. I'm going to the supermarket. Is there anything special you want me to get?

Sunny   What's on the list so far, Dad?

Father   Just a _____ of beans.

Jay   Well, we need a _____ of jam.

Sunny   Can you get a _____ of soda?

Father   Sure. What kind, Sunny?

Sunny   Coke or Pepsi. It doesn't matter.

Father   All right. What else?

Jay   We need some cereal, Dad.

Sunny   Okay, Jay. A _____ of cereal.

Father   We also need a _____ of flour.

Sunny   And we need some bread, Dad. Can you get a _____ of white bread and two loaves of whole wheat bread?

Father Sure. And I'm going to get a _____ of bananas and two bunches of carrots.

Sunny Good idea, Dad.

Jay We also need a _____ of lettuce.

Father All right.

Jay And can you get a _____ of butter and maybe a half pound of cheese?

Father Okay.

Sunny We need another _____ of milk, Dad.

Father All right.

Jay And a _____ eggs.

Father Okay. Anything else?

Sunny No. That's it.

Jay I can't think of anything else.

Father Okay. Let me see if I have everything here. That's a can of beans, a _____ of jam, a bottle of soda, a box of cereal, a bag of flour, a loaf of white bread, two _____ of whole wheat bread, a bunch of bananas, two bunches of carrots, a _____ of lettuce, a pound of butter, and a half pound of cheese, a _____ of milk, and a dozen eggs, Is that it?

Sunny   That's everything, Dad.

Father   Okay. I'll see you kids later.

Jay   That's a pretty long shopping list, Dad. Do you want me to go with you?

Father   Sure, Jay. I'd love it.

Sunny   I'm not busy right now, Dad. I can go, too.

Father   Great!

Jay   Let's go!

Compare your answers.

Jay   What are you writing, Dad?

Father   A shopping list. I'm going to the supermarket. Is there anything special you want me to get?

Sunny   What's on the list so far, Dad?

Father   Just a can of beans.

Jay   Well, we need a jar of jam.

Sunny   Can you get a bottle of soda?

Father   Sure. What kind, Sunny?

Sunny   Coke or Pepsi. It doesn't matter.

Father   All right. What else?

Jay	We need some cereal, Dad.
Sunny	Okay, Jay. A _box_ of cereal.
Father	We also need a bag of flour.
Sunny	And we need some bread, Dad. Can you get a _loaf_ of white bread and two loaves of whole wheat bread?
Father	Sure. And I'm going to get a _bunch_ of bananas and two bunches of carrots.
Sunny	Good idea, Dad.
Jay	We also need a _head_ of lettuce.
Father	All right.
Jay	And can you get a _pound_ of butter and maybe a half pound of cheese?
Father	Okay.
Sunny	We need another _quart_ of milk, Dad.
Father	All right.
Jay	And a _dozen_ eggs.
Father	Okay. Anything else?
Sunny	No. That's it.
Jay	I can't think of anything else.
Father	Okay. Let me see if I have everything here. That's a can

of beans, a _jar_ of jam, a bottle of soda, a box of cereal, a bag of flour, a loaf of white bread, two _loaves_ of whole wheat bread, a bunch of bananas, two bunches of carrots, a head of lettuce, a pound of butter, and a half pound of cheese, a _quart_ of milk, and a dozen eggs, Is that it?

Sunny   That's everything, Dad.

Father   Okay. I'll see you kids later.

Jay   That's a pretty long shopping list, Dad. Do you want me to go with you?

Father   Sure, Jay. I'd love it.

Sunny   I'm not busy right now, Dad. I can go, too.

Father   Great!

Jay   Let's go!

2) Exercises for Delicious Desserts

* Circle the right one.

1. **a piece of**

    a. apple pie   b. ice cream   c. coffee

2. **a slice of**

    a. pudding   b. cheesecake   c. apple

3. **a bowl of**

    a. strawberries   b. cheesecake   c. tea

4. **a dish of**

    a. chocolate cake   b. tea   c. vanilla ice cream

5. **a cup of**

    a. blueberries   b. coffee   c. milk

6. **a glass of**

    a. milk   b. strawberries   c. pudding

Part 2 — **Culinary English**

1. Recipe Reading & Writing Exercise (레시피 연습)

• Raisin Cake

Here is a recipe for how to make a raisin cake. Read the recipe and answer the questions. Read the questions carefully.

Recipe for 4 people

1. Heat the oven to gas mark 5.

2. Mix the butter and sugar.

3. Add the eggs and flour.

4. Stir in the raisins.

5. Put the ingredients into the baking tin.

6. Bake in the oven for 35 minutes.

Questions

1. What are the ingredients you need to make this cake?

2. Which temperature should you heat the oven to?

3. How long should you bake the cake for?

4. How many people is the cake for?

* Underline all of the verbs in the recipe.

Circle the right one.

This cake is overcooked! You'd better preheat the _____ ten minutes to 120°C before putting it in, instead of twenty minutes.

a. freezer   b. toaster   c. oven

2. About Eggs

Q: How would you like your egg?

A: I'd like it scrambled, please.

egg shell	egg white	egg yolk
계란 껍질	계란 흰자	계란 노른자
hard-boiled egg	soft-boiled egg	fried egg
완숙 계란	반숙 계란	계란 프라이

sunny-side up 한 면만 익힌 반숙 프라이	**over easy** 양면을 흰자만 익힌 반숙 프라이	**over hard** 양면을 노른자까지 익힌 완숙 프라이
turned over 뒤집은 계란 요리	**poached egg** 수란	**steamed egg** 계란 찜
egg garnish 지단	**boil an egg** 계란을 삶다	**beat the egg** 계란을 풀다
cook an egg 계란을 조리하다	**separate the egg white and yolk** 흰자 노른자를 분리하다	**egg slicer** 계란 썰기

3. My Favorite Recipe (내가 좋아하는 레시피)

• Scrambled Egg (serves 2)

Ingredients

6ea	eggs
2g	salt
pinch	pepper
30ml	milk
15ml	clarified butter

Directions

1. **Beat** the eggs with a whisk and add milk.

2. **Grease** the pan with **clarified butter**.

3. Pour the egg **mixture** into the pan.

4. Cook the eggs in a pan.

5. Season with salt and pepper.

6. Check the consistency.

4. Cuisine Quiz (조리 퀴즈)

1. Oil should be added to the greens in a salad before the vinegar.

    a. True   b. False

2. Why should the chef split the broccoli stems?

    a. So the broccoli will have a more attractive appearance.
    b. So the stems would cook faster.

UNIT 6 Breakfast, Lunch & Dinner

Part 1 · English Skill Up

1. Vocabulary Preview
2. Classroom Activities
3. Dialogues
4. English for Fun

Part 2 · Culinary English

1. Recipe Reading & Writing Exercise(레시피 연습)
2. Cutting Vegetables(야채 썰기)
3. About Knife(칼)
4. My Favorite Recipe(내가 좋아하는 레시피)
5. Cuisine Quiz(조리 퀴즈)

Part 1 — English Skill Up

1. Vocabulary Preview 🎧

1) Breakfast

bacon	
bagel	
butter	
cereal	
cereal bowl	
cocoa	
cream	cream cheese
Danish	French toast
egg	grits
home fries	jam
jelly	margarine
milk	muffin
oatmeal	orange juice
pancakes	sugar
syrup	salami

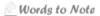

Words to Note

salami	grits
이탈리아식 말린 소시지	미국 남부에서 많이 먹는 옥수수죽

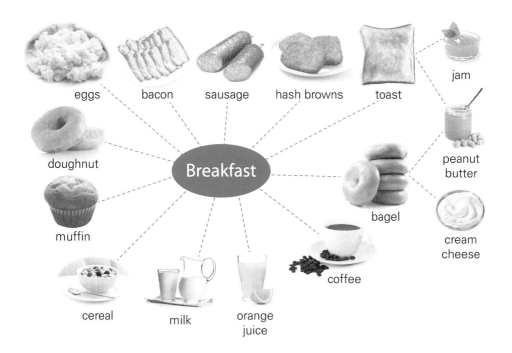

eggs bacon sausage hash browns toast jam

doughnut **Breakfast** peanut butter

muffin bagel cream cheese

cereal milk orange juice coffee

2) Lunch

cafeteria	
cheese	
coffee mug	
cold cuts	
frozen entree	
ham sandwich	
hero (submarine/ grinder)	ketchup
leftovers	lunch box
lunchroom	mayonnaise
microwave oven	mustard
peanut butter	plastic baggie

potato chips	roast beef sandwich
roll	salad
salami	sandwich
slice of bread	soup
spaghetti	spaghetti sauce
thermos	yogurt

Words to Note

Sub Sandwich : Hero, Submarine, Sub, Wedge, Grinder, Baguette 등 여러 이름으로 불린다. 지하철 의미의 subway가 아니라 Submarine(잠수함)의 약칭. 기다란 롤빵에 얹은 샌드위치 모양이 잠수함 같

다고 불러진 이름. 1950년대 뉴욕 시 주위에서 Hero라는 이름으로 시작. 뉴잉글랜드 지역에서는 입을 크게 벌려 이빨로 우직우직 씹어 먹는다는 의미로 Grinder라고 불림. 또한 롤빵을 벌려 내용물을 쐐기(wedge) 모양으로 집어넣는다는 의미로 Wedge로도 불림.

leftovers : 남은 음식

thermos : 보온병, 써모스 그룹에서 제조한 보온병 브랜드

3) Dinner

ash tray

beer

busboy

check

glass of water

hostess

maitre d'

restaurant

smoking section

waiter

wine

nonsmoking section

restroom

tip

waitress

2. Classroom Activities

Partner Interview

Partner's Name: _____

* Practice these questions with your teacher and partner.

Q1. What is a typical breakfast for you?

Q2. What time do you eat breakfast?

Q3. Do you eat breakfast with your family?

Q4. Do you eat breakfast at home?

Q5. In your opinion, what is a healthy breakfast?

Group Survey

- Ask everyone in your group these questions.
- Check ALWAYS, SOMETIMES, or NEVER.
- Count the answers.
- Report your group's results to the class.
- Write the class' results on the board.

How often do you _____.

	How often do you _____ ?	ALWAYS	SOMETIMES	NEVER
1	skip breakfast?			
2	drink coffee for breakfast?			
3	have cold cereal for breakfast?			
4	have got cereal for breakfast?			
5	have fruit or juice for breakfast?			
6	have something sweet for breakfast?			
7	eat out for breakfast?			
8	eat a nutritious breakfast?			

3. Dialogues 🎧

Dialogue 1

A What do you eat for breakfast, Paul?

B Not much, really. Usually I have a glass of orange juice and vitamins. I always take vitamins in the morning.

A Do you eat anything else for breakfast?

B Sometimes I have a piece of toast.

C I always have a big breakfast: eggs, bacon, home fries, coffee, and juice. I love American breakfasts.

A I do, too, Sam, but they make me fat.

C What do you eat for breakfast, Kathy?

A I have juice, **nonfat** yogurt, and toast. It's better for my health.

Notes nonfat 탈지된

Dialogue 2

A Dialogue Squares again! OK, first we write our own answers.

B I wrote my answers already.

C Me, too.

A All right. Let's ask the questions, then. What did you have for breakfast today, Van Yen?

B I had noodle soup.

A Noodle soup! Really?

B Oh, yes. It's very good. I always have noodle soup for breakfast. What did you have, Jack?

A Hot cereal and cocoa. It's my favorite in the winter. I have it every day. What about you, Mimi?

C Just a cup of coffee. I never eat anything for breakfast.

A So we each have the same breakfast every day.

C Yes, but we don't all have the same breakfast!

Dialogue 3

A I'm so hungry! I **skipped** lunch today, and now I'm really hungry!

B I never skip lunch, Ken.

A Well, I'm sorry I did. What did you have for lunch, Jim?

B Spaghetti and meatballs.

A That sounds wonderful! Where did you go for lunch?

B Oh, I just ate at work. We have a **microwave oven** there. I always bring in **leftovers** and warm them up.

A That's a good idea. Do you like to cook?

B No, but my mother is a great cook. She always makes lots of food, and I have leftovers for lunch.

A Lucky you! Does your mother want another son?

Notes   skip 빼먹다   microwave oven 전자레인지
leftover 남은 음식

Dialogue 4

A What's for lunch, Paco?

B Sandwiches.

A Oh, good. I love sandwiches.

B What would you like on yours, Maria?

A What do you have?

B Everything — **cold cuts**, tuna fish, cheese, peanut butter - you name it! We have three kinds of bread, too.

A Great! Do you have sliced turkey?

B Sure do. What kind of bread? White? Wheat? **Rye**?

A Rye, please. And could I have some lettuce, tomato, and mayonnaise with that?

B You bet.

A What a beautiful sandwich! Thanks, Paco.

Notes cold cuts 런천미트, 샌드위치햄, 쿡트미트 등의 육가공품들
rye 호밀

Dialogue 5

A I'm glad we came to this restaurant, David. It's beautiful!

B It is nice, isn't it? Margaret, there's something I want to talk to you about.

A Really? What is it, David?

B Well, we've known each other for three years now.

A Uh-huh.

B And we like each other... a lot.

A Yes, we do.

B Well, I...

C David! Margaret! What a surprise! Hey, Annie, it's David and Margaret! Oh, this is great! Let's have dinner together!

D Wait, Jack. Maybe David and Margaret want to eat alone.

B No, no... That's... That's fine, Annie. It's... it's good to see you, really.

4. English for Fun

1) Reading: Healthy Breakfast 🎧

Mr. and Mrs. Jones are on a diet. They are trying to lose weight. Mr. Jones has high cholesterol, and Mrs. Jones has gained weight. Their doctor told them to start exercising and eating healthier foods. He told them to eat cereal or oatmeal each morning for breakfast instead of bacon and eggs.

Now, Mr. Jones eats cereal with low-fat milk for breakfast, and Mrs. Jones eats oatmeal. They miss eating a big breakfast, but they are sticking to their diets. After breakfast, Mr. and Mrs. Jones take their dogs for a walk. Walking is a good exercise

2) Reading: Unhealthy Breakfast 🎧

Jack is a bachelor. He works in downtown Chicago as a shoe salesman. Every morning on his way to work, Jack stops at a donut shop and buys a chocolate donut and a cup of coffee. Jack likes this morning routine because it is quick and easy. He doesn't have to cook breakfast or wash the dishes.

Last time Jack went to the doctor for a checkup his doctor told him that he had high cholesterol. The doctor told Jack to stop eating foods that are high in fat. Donuts are fried in a lot of fat.

※ True or False

1.   Jack is a shoe salesman in Seattle, Washington.

2.   Jack is married, but he and his wife are getting a divorce.

3.   The nurse told Jack to stop eating fatty foods like donuts.

4.   In the picture, Jack is sitting on a stool and drinking coffee.

5.   Donuts are healthy because they are fried in fat.

Part 2 — Culinary English

1. Recipe Reading & Writing Exercise (레시피 연습)

• Chef's Salad

A. Read this recipe for a chef's salad and fill in the gaps with the words given.

add	boil	cut	mix	pour	put	remove	serve	slice	salad

Instructions

1.   the eggs for 10 minutes.

2.   up the lettuce leaves and put them into a salad bowl. Cut the cheese and the ham into small pieces and add them to the bowl.

3.   the cucumber and cut the tomato into pieces, then add them to the bowl.

4.   the shell from the eggs, slice them and put them on top of the

5.

For the dressing

6. _____ the mayonnaise, tomato ketchup, olive oil and vinegar into a small bowl and _____ .

7. _____ them well.

8. _____ salt and pepper.

Finally, 9. _____ the dressing over the salad.

10. _____ with fresh bread.

Chef's Salad

Ingredients
2 eggs

8 lettuce leaves

150g Edam cheese

4 slices ham

1 small cucumber

1 large tomato

Dressing
2 tablespoons mayonnaise

1 tablespoon tomato ketchup

1 tablespoon vinegar

1 tablespoon olive oil

Salt and pepper

B. Now say if the following sentences are (T) or (F)?

1. You need two eggs to make a chef's salad.　　(T)　　(F)

2. Boil the eggs for 15 minutes.　　(T)　　(F)

3. Cut the cheese and the ham into big pieces.　(T)　　(F)

4. Cut the tomato into pieces.　　(T)　　(F)

5. Serve with fresh vegetables.　　(T)　　(F)

2. Cutting Vegetables (야채 썰기)

야채 썰기의 방법은 매우 다양하나 다음의 가장 기본적인 방법 일곱 가지는 요리 학교를 나온 전문가가 아닐지라도 꼭 마스터하여야 한다.

Seven Vegetable Cuts Every Cook Should Master

출처 http://culinary.utk.edu/7-vegetable-cuts-every-cook-master

1) Rough Chop (대충 잘게 자르기)

가장 기본적인 야채 썰기 방법. 특별한 제약 없이 3/4인치 내지 1인치 정도 크기로 그야말로 대충(roughly) 써는 방법이다. 레시피에서 야채를 어떻게 썰어라는 지시가 없다면 셰프들은 재료들을 반으로 또 더 작은 조각으로 대충 자르기를 한다. 볶음 요리 등에서 양파, 피망, 애호박 등을 썰 때 사용된다.

2) Dice (주사위 모양 자르기)

주사위 모양의 네모로 써는 방법(대략 가로, 세로 1cm). 감자, 토마토, 양파, 피망에 흔히 쓰임.

   ① Large dice (3/4 inch)

   ② Medium dice (1/2 inch)

   ③ Small dice (1/4 inch)

3) Mince (곱게 다지기)

Mince는 Chop보다 훨씬 가늘게 다지는 것이다(마늘 등). 다진 야채는 빨리 익으므로 육수나 소스 만들 때에 좋다.

4) Slice (슬라이스, 편으로 썰기)

가장 일반적인 썰기로 납작하게 편으로 얇게 써는 방법이다. 두께는 레시피에 지시하는 대로 감자칩 같은 경우에는 얇게 썰고, 가지 요리를 할 때는 보다 두껍게 썬다.

5) Julienne (줄리안느, 채썰기)

Julienne(줄리안느)는 가끔 성냥개비썰기 (matchstick cut) 혹은 구두끈모양썰기(shoe string)라고도 불린다. 길이는 2.5~5cm, 너비는 0.15cm 정도 되는 가는 네모 막대형의 야채썰기 형태이며, 당근, 무, 감자, 셀러리 등을 조리할 때 자주 쓰인다.

6) Brunoise (브뤼누아즈)

Brunoise(브뤼누아즈)는 기본적으로 줄리안느 썰기를 먼저 한 후 정육면체 썰기를 하는 것이다. Dice보다 더 작은 정육면체 네모썰기이다. 즉 0.3 × 0.3 × 0.3 cm 정도로 가장 작은 정육면체 썰기이다.

7) Chiffonade (쉬포나드)

Chiffonade(쉬포나드)는 실처럼 가늘게 써는 것이다. 바질 잎이나 상추 잎 등 주로 허브 잎을 겹겹이 쌓은 다음 둥글게 말아서 실처럼 가늘게 썬다.

그 외 중요한 썰기 방법

❶ Batonne(바토네)(=Large Julienne) : 성냥개비보다 굵게 재목처럼 자르는 방법. 네모 막대형 썰기. 가로, 세로 및 길이가 각각 1.3 × 1.3 × 6cm 두께로 길게 네모 막대형으로 썰기.

❷ Allumette(알루메트)(=Medium Julienne) : 가로, 세로 및 길이가 각각 0.3 × 0.3 × 5~6cm의 성냥개비 크기 정도 채썰기, 바토네보다 가로 세로가 더 짧다.

❸ Paysanne(페이상) : 장방형 모양으로 가로, 세로 1cm 크기로 얇게 자르거나 혹은 삼각형으로 자르는 방법

❹ Chateau(샤토) : 프랑스 말로 성(城)이라는 뜻이며 타원형으로 각각의 면이 나타나도록 양끝을 자르는 오크(Oak)통 모양이며, 당근, 무, 감자, 호박 등에 사용한다.

❺ Olivette(올리베트) : 샤토와 비슷한 형태이나 양끝이 뾰족한 올리브 모양이며, 주로 감자나 당근 등을 가니쉬로 사용할 때 이용된다.

❻ Parisienne(파리지엥) : 둥글고 작은 구슬형으로 스쿠프(Scoop)나 볼러(Baller)를 이용하며, 둥글게 돌려가면서 떼어낸다. 고명이나 모양, 장식을 할 때 이용된다.

❼ Turning(터닝) : 돌리면서 모양을 내는 것으로 사과 등의 과일을 깎거나 삶은 감자(Boiled potatoes) 등에 이용된다. 초보 조리사들이 먼저 익혀야 할 기본적인 기능이다.

❽ Concasse(콩카세) : 토마토 껍질을 벗긴 다음 씨앗을 제거하고 가로, 세로 각 0.5cm 정도의 크기의 정사각형으로 써는 것. 가니쉬나 소스로 많이 사용한다.

1. 칼을 이용하여 돌려가면서 깎는 자르기 방법은?

2. Chop이 자주 사용되는 채소는?

3. 한국어로 '채썰기'를 영어로 무엇이라 하는가?

4. 한국어로 '깍둑썰기'를 영어로 무엇이라 하는가?

5. 야채 잎들을 겹겹이 쌓고 둥글게 말아서 실처럼 써는 것을 무엇이라 하는가?

Answers

1. 터닝 2. 양파, 파마늘 등 3. Julienne 4. dice 5. chiffonade

3. About Knife

• Chef's knife (셰프 나이프)

A chef's knife is another name of French knife. It is a cutting knife used in food preparation. The use of chef's knife is to slice vegetables and disjoint large cuts of meats in small pieces

셰프 나이프는 프렌치 나이프의 다른 이름이다. 음식 준비에서 사용되는 칼이다. 셰프 나이프는 야채를 자르고 고기 큰 토막들을 작은 조각들로 분해하는 데 사용된다.

The Parts of a Knife (칼의 각 부분의 명칭)

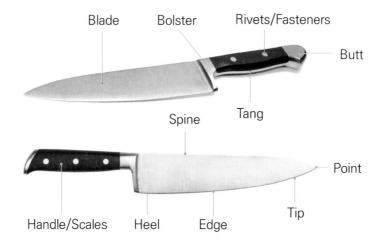

- **Point, Tip(포인트, 팁) 칼끝** : 작은 재료나 정교한 칼질을 할 때 사용

- **Spine(스파인) 칼등** : 우리나라의 식칼은 대개 외날이다. 등과 날이 칼끝으로 향하면서 완만한 곡선을 이루고 칼등이 칼날에 비해 두껍다.

- **Blade(블레이드), (Cutting) Edge 칼날** : 재료를 썰 때 주로 사용.

- **Bloster(볼스터) 지지대** : 손잡이와 칼 몸통을 잇는 받침, 칼질을 할 때 손가락과 칼날의 거리를 적당히 유지하게 한다.

- **Handle(핸들) 손잡이** : 탱이 붙어 있는 칼의 손잡이 부분.

- **Heel(힐) 칼 뒤축** : 무, 셀러리 뿌리 부분 등 딱딱한 재료를 썰 때 힘이 들어감.

- **Tang(탱) 손잡이 속의 강철** : 이 곳의 길이가 적당해야 칼의 균형이 잘 맞음.

- **Rivets(리벳), fastener, 대갈못** : 못으로 단단히 연결된 부위.

4. My Favorite Recipe (내가 좋아하는 레시피)

• Broccoli Soup (serves 2)

Ingredients

1 tablespoon grapeseed oil

1 ea   onion, halved and sliced

3 cups chicken stock

1 broccoli ① florets separated, ② stems peeled, cut into medium dices

tt   salt and pepper

Directions

1. In a saucepan, heat the grapeseed oil over medium heat.

2. Add onion and cook until softened for 5 minutes.

3. Stir in the chicken stock and broccoli florets and stem rounds.

4. Bring to a boil and reduce the heat. Simmer until the broccoli is tender for about 10 minutes.

5. Puree the soup using a blender. Return the soup to the pot and season with salt and pepper. Serve Immediately.

5. Cuisine Quiz (조리 퀴즈)

1. What are the most important concerns in cooking vegetables?

   a. To avoid overcooking.

   b. To preserve nutritional value, color, and add some flavor.

   c. Both of these.

2. The acids cause many green vegetables to lose their natural color in cooking. To preserve the color of green vegetables, they should be boiled   .

   a. Covered   b. Uncovered

UNIT 7

Dessert, Fast Food & Junk Food

Part 1 · English Skill Up

1. Vocabulary Preview
2. Classroom Activities
3. Dialogues
4. English for Fun

Part 2 · Culinary English

1. Recipe Reading & Writing Exercise(레시피 연습)
2. Weights, Measures and Temperatures
3. My Favorite Recipe(내가 좋아하는 레시피)
4. Cuisine Quiz(조리 퀴즈)

Part 1 — English Skill Up

1. Vocabulary Preview 🎧

1) Dessert

beverage	
brownie	
cake	
candy	
cappuccino	
cheesecake	
coffee	coffeecake
cone	cookies
doughnut	espresso
frozen yogurt	ice cream
ice cream soda	iced coffee
iced tea	lemonade
milk shake	pastry
pie	pie a la mode
sherbet	sundae
tea	

✏️ *Words to Note*

- pie a la mode : 아이스크림을 얹은 파이

- sherbet : 셔벗, 과즙에 설탕, 얼음, 물을 탄 청량음료

- sundae : 선데이, 선디

  💬 아이스크림 선디 : 길다란 유리잔에 아이스크림을 넣고 시럽, 견과류, 과일 조각 등을 얹은 것

2) Fast Food

bun	
cashier	
cash register	
change	
chicken nuggets	
counter	
customer	drive-in/ drive-thru window
hamburger	hot sauce (salsa)
line	order
pay	pickle
salad	bar
salad dressing	shake
soft drink	straw

✎ *Words to Note*

• bun : 번빵. 쪽진 머리(bun)처럼 작고 동글납작한 빵

bun

mustard   sausage

hambuger   chicken patty   veggie burger   hotdog

filling

sandwich   club sandwich   open-face sandwich   wrap

sauce   savory   sweet

topping

kebab   chicken nuggets

crepes

fish and chips   ribs   fried chicken   pizza

출처 https://www.easypacelearning.com/design/images/typesfcooked%20food.jpg

3) Junkfood

bubble gum

candy bar

cheese snack

chocolate bar

corn chips

crackers

gum

peanuts

pretzels

soda

vending machine

juice drink

popcorn

snack machine

tortilla chips

✎ *Words to Note*

pretzel
프레첼

vending machine
자동판매기

2. Classroom Activities

Group Discussion

Work in groups of five.

Discuss these questions.

Report your answers to the class

Q1. What is your favorite dessert?

Q2. Do you buy it or prepare it?

Q3. Is it fattening?

Q4. How often do you have your favorite dessert?

Group Survey

Ask everyone in your group these questions.

Check YES or NO.

Count the answers.

Report your group's results on the board.

	Do you _____?	YES	NO
1	ever eat fast foods?		
2	like hamburgers with "everything"?		
3	like French fries?		
4	like ketchup on your fries?		
5	like chicken nuggets?		
6	like hot dogs?		

7	like mustard on your hot dogs?
8	like soft drinks?
9	like salsa?
10	think fast food is bad for you?

3. Dialogues 🎧

Dialogue 1

A How do we do this activity?

B First, we **fill in** the menu with desserts we all like.

c I'll start with brownies. And what about the prices?

D Let's fill in all the desserts first, and then do the prices.

B OK. How about apple pie with ice cream?

A That's called apple pie a la mode. Let's add sherbet.

c And **frozen** yogurt. That's popular these days.

D How many desserts do we have now?

A Four. We need one more. How about some chocolate chip cookies?

B Great! The menu's ready. Oh, wait a minute! We didn't do the prices!

(Bell rings.)

Notes fill in 기입해 넣다　　　　　frozen 냉동된
That's it for today. 오늘은 여기까지입니다.

Dialogue 2

A This looks like a great class! Look at all those desserts!

B Here's the dessert I brought in. It's called "anpan." It's a pastry filled with **red bean paste**. It's from Japan.

C That looks delicious. Mine is from Puerto Rico. It's "**flan**."

D Well, look at mine! It looks the same. It's called "**crème brûlée**" and is very popular in France.

C It does look the same as mine! What's in it?

D It's made with milk and eggs. It's a custard.

C It is the same! I can't wait to taste it!

Teacher I know you are all waiting for this: break time!

Students Oh, great! Delicious! Mmm! Wonderful!

red bean paste   팥죽

flan   플랜: 계란, 치즈, 과일 등을 넣은 파이

créme brûlée   크렘 브릴레: 녹인 설탕을 위에 얹은 크림. 캐러멜로 만든
설탕 크림 디저트

Dialogue 3

A   Do you think fast food is bad for you, Heather?

B   Yes, of course. I like fast food, but I know
it's bad for me.

A   OK, that's it! We're finished with the
Group Survey Questions.

C   Now we count the answers, right?

A   Right. I have four "yesses" and three "nos" for
Number 1.

B   No, that's not right! I have three "yesses" and four
"nos."

C   And I have four "yesses" and four "nos"

D   That can't be right. There are only seven people in our
group. What do we do now?

C   Count again. Or ask the questions again, raise our
hands, and count together.

A, B, D   Oh, boy! Not again!

Dialogue 4

A Role plays are difficult to write, aren't they?

B Do you think so? I think they're easy.

A Easy? Really? I'm glad you're my partner, Victor.

B OK. Let's see now... The cashier says "May I help you?"

A Why doesn't he say "Can I help you?"

B Because it says "May I help you" in the book.

A But is "Can I help you?" OK? I hear people say "Can I help you?" in stores all the time.

B Yes, That's true. You can say that. But I think "May I help you?" is a little more polite.

A Really? But, can we change it, anyway?

B: I think I understand why role plays are difficult for you to write, Lisa.

Notes role play 역할놀이

Dialogue 5

A **Coffee break**! Junk food time! I'm going to the vending machines. Want something, Bob?

B No thanks, Mary.

A Don't you ever eat junk food?

B Not from these **vending machines**!

A Why not?

B Last week I lost money in the machine three times! Nothing came out — no soda, no coffee, no money back.

A That's too bad! What did you do?

B I kicked the machine a few times, but nothing happened.

A Well, I hope it works today. I'm really hungry for a chocolate bar! Wish me luck!

| Notes | coffee break 커피 휴식시간 | vending machine 자동판매기 |

4. English for Fun

1) Reading 🎧

An Interesting Story

A man who had been married for ten years was consulting a marriage counselor. "When I was first married, I was very happy. I'd come home from a hard day, and my little dog would race around barking, and my wife would bring me my slippers. Now everything's changed. When I come home, my dog brings me my slippers, and my wife barks at me."

"I don't know what your're complaining about," said the counselor. "You're still getting the same service."

2) Food Quiz

1. ginger ale   2. chewing gum   3. coffee
4. spaghetti   5. croissant   6. hamburger

Match the foods with the countries of their origin.

a. Germany

b. Ethiopia

c. Mexico

d. China

e. Austria

f. Ireland

Part 2 — Culinary English

1. Recipe Reading & Writing Exercise (레시피 연습)

• Potato Salad Recipe

Read the following recipe.

Ingredients

potatoes

6 hard boiled eggs

mayonnaise

purple onion

orange peppers

broccoli

celery

Directions

1. Peel the potatoes and boil them.
2. Rinse the cooked potatoes in cold water and let cool.
3. Chop the potatoes into small pieces.
4. Boil the eggs.
5. Peel and chop the hard-boiled eggs.
6. Combine the potatoes and the eggs in a pot.
7. Chop the vegetables and mix into the pot slowly.
8. Mix the mayo into the salad slowly.
9. Salt to taste.

Now match the cooking actions below to the pictures.

a. chop   b. salt   c. peel   d. mix   e. rinse   f. combine   g. boil

2. Weights, Measures and Temperatures (무게, 도량형, 온도)

레시피에는 미터법과 파운드법이 동시에 사용되므로, 이를 포괄적으로 이해해 요리 계량 시 적용하여야 한다. 아래 약어 표현이 레시피에 자주 나오는 것들이므로 숙지해 두어야 한다.

1) Abbreviations (약어)

metric	Imperial and American
g gram	**oz** ounce
kg kilogram	**lb** pound
dl deciliter	**fl oz** fluid ounce
liter this is always given in full	**pt** pint
mm millimeter	**gal** gallon
cm centimeter	**in** inch
	tsp teaspoon(작은 숟갈)
	tbs tablespoon(큰 숟갈)

the U.S cup = 8 fluid ounces

the U.S pint = 2 cups or 16 fl oz

the U.S gallon = 8 U.S. pints or 128 fl oz

1 oz = 25g

1 lb = 450g

ea : each(개, 개수) ex) 1 ea of bay leaf(월계수 잎 하나)

pc : piece(조각, 쪽) ex) 1 piece of apple

ph : pinch(조금, 약간), 엄지와 검지 사이의 양으로 소금, 설탕 등의 분말
을 측정 ex) a pinch of salt

sl : slice(슬라이스) ex) slices of onion

cl : clove(조각, 쪽) ex) a clove of garlic(마늘 한 조각)

bn : bundle, bunch(다발, 묶음) ex) a bundle of celery

c : cp : cup(컵) : C = 240g

inch : 1인치 = 2.54cm

2) Conversion (계량단위 환산기준, 미터법과 파운드법의 환산)

$\frac{1}{2}$oz = 14 grams

1 oz = 28.3 grams

10 ozs = 283 grams

1 tablespoon = 15mL

1 cup = 8ozs = 0.23 liter = 230g

1 pint = 470 mL = 약 2 cup

$\frac{3}{4}$oz = 21 grams

2ozs = 57 grams

1 teaspoon = $\frac{1}{3}$ tablespoon

1 tablespoon = 3 teaspoon

1 gallon = 4 quart = 16 cup

1 lb = 453 grs, 2 lbs = 905 grams

3) 화씨와 섭씨의 상관관계

Temperatures

C : Celsius or Centigrade   **F** : Fahrenheit

- 섭씨(℃)에서 화씨(℉)로 변환 : (섭씨 × 1.8) + 32
- 화씨(℉)에서 섭씨(℃)로 변환 : (화씨 − 32) / 1.8

Q 물의 온도가 100이다, 화씨로는 몇 도인가?

A ℉ = (100×1.8) + 32 = 212

Check about Measures

아래 빈칸을 채우시오.

1. 1C = (g)
2. 1T = (t)
3. 1L = (g)
4. 1oz = (g)
5. 50℃ = (℉)
6. 100℉ = (℃)

3. My Favorite Recipe (내가 좋아하는 레시피)

• Balsamic Vinaigrette (Makes 500ml)

Vinaigrette is a culinary sauce made by mixing vinegar and oil and usually seasoning it with salt, herbs and/or spices. It is made by mixing oil with something acidic such as vinegar or lemon juice. The mixture can be enhanced with salt. It is used most commonly as a salad dressing.

Ingredients

12ml	balsamic vinegar
360ml	olive oil
Pinch	sugar
1tsp	mustard
Tt	salt and black pepper
Pinch	dried basil

Directions

1. In a bowl, combine the **vinegar**, sugar, mustard, salt and pepper. Gradually **whisk** in oil.

2. Check the **seasoning** with salt and pepper, if necessary. Mix in dried basil.

3. Serve immediately or store in the refrigerator for later use.

Notes   vinegar   식초   whisk   휘젓다

seasoning   양념 조미료

4. Cuisine Quiz (조리 퀴즈)

1. How can you help others avoid being burned?

   a. Keep your mind on the job.

   b. Warn others when something is hot.

   c. Both.

2. Keep knives in the proper storage space when not in use. If you have to lay the knife down for a minute, be sure it is

   a. Tucked away where it can't be seen.

   b. On a cutting board.

   c. In plain view.

3. The reason you should always slice or chop food on a cutting board is

   a. Cutting on wood keeps the blade from slipping.

   b. Cutting on metal, tile, or other composition surfaces won't keep the blade from slipping.

   c. Both of these.

Answers

1. b   2. c

3. c

I'm
Kitchen
English

CHAPTER 3

Cuisine English

Unit·8 Salads
Unit·9 Soups
Unit·10 Seafood
Unit·11 Bread
Unit·12 Roasting
Unit·13 Broiling

학습목표

샐러드, 수프, 야채, 생선요리, 빵의 기본 지식 및 여러 가지 요리법을 터득하여 요리에 관한 영어 원서를 해석하고 활용할 수 있는 능력을 기른다. 모든 메뉴를 이해하여 국제적으로 표준화된 조리사 양성에 도움이 될 수 있게 한다.

UNIT 8 · Salads

Part 1 · English Skill Up

1. Vocabulary Preview
2. Reading
3. Review Exercises
4. English for Fun

Part 2 · Culinary English

1. Recipe Reading & Writing Exercise(레시피 연습)
2. Kitchen Equipment(주방 장비)(1)
3. Cuisine Quiz(조리 퀴즈)

Part 1 — English Skill Up

1. Vocabulary Preview 🎧

definition	정의	vinegar	식초
acid	산	seasoning	조미료, 양념
dressed	드레싱을 입힌	occidental	서양의 (반: oriental)
emulsion	유액	starch	녹말
thickener	진하게 만드는 것	expert	전문가
adhere	달라붙다	tear	찢다
bruise	손상되다		

2. Reading 🎧

SALADS

1) The definition of salad

We usually think of a salad as a cold dish of greens or other vegetables dressed with oil and vinegar.

2) Three basic salad dressings

(1) French dressing

It is one of the simplest and most widely used of dressings. It consists of oil and vinegar or other acid liquids such as lemon juice or fruit juice, plus seasonings.

(2) Mayonnaise

It is also one of the basic dressings, popular over the occidental worlds. It is an emulsion of eggs, vinegar or lemon juice, oil and seasonings.

(3) Boiled (cooked) salad dressing

Of dressings this is the only one which is thickened with a starch. The liquid used in this dressing may be milk, vinegar or fruit juice, water or other liquid. Eggs are added too as a thickener.

• Reading Helper

1) 샐러드의 정의

기름, 식초로 만든 야채 요리

2) 세 가지 기본 샐러드 드레싱

❶ French dressing : 가장 간단하고 보편적 드레싱. 기름, 식초에 레몬주스, 과일주스 등 산성 액체와 양념을 가한 것

❷ Mayonnaise : 서양의 가장 기본적인 드레싱. 계란 유액, 식초, 레몬주스, 기름, 양념 등

❸ Boiled(cooked) salad dressing : 끓이거나 조리한 샐러드 드레싱, 녹말풀로 단단하게 만든 것, 우유, 식초, 과일주스, 물, 계란은 뻑뻑하게 하기 위한 것

• More about Salad and Dressing (샐러드와 드레싱 보충자료)

1) Salad (샐러드)

샐러드란 라틴어 'Sal'에서 유래한 말이다. '싱싱한 야채를 주재료로 하여 소금을 가미한 것'이라는 뜻을 지니고 있다. 요즘에는 야채뿐 아니라 육류, 과일, 생선도 첨가하여 드레싱과 함께 제공하기도 한다. 기원전 그리스, 로마시대부터 시작된 것으로 보이며, 본래는 약초에 해당하는 마늘, 파슬리, 셀러리, 물냉이(크레송)와 같은 것을 재료로 하여 소화흡수에 도움이 되게 한 것으로 보인다. 비프스테이크, 로스트비프 등 산성식품인 육류 요리에 알칼리성 생 채소를 곁들여 먹음으로써 입맛이 개운해서 좋고 영양상 균형이 잡히며 소화 흡수에 효과적이어서, 산성식품에 대한 필수식품으로 널리 애용된다. 보통 샐러드는 프랑스식으로는 앙트레 다음 코스로 서빙되나 요즘에는 미국식으로 앙트레 직전에 서빙되기도 한다.

샐러드의 종류

(1) 순수 샐러드(Simple Salad)
믹스 샐러드(Mixed Salad) : 여러가지 야채를 혼합하여 만든 샐러드

계절 샐러드(Seasonal Salad) : 계절감에 부합하는 야채를 이용하여 만든 샐러드

시저 샐러드(Caesar Salad) : 로마시대 시저가 즐겨 먹던 샐러드로서, 고객의 기호에 맞는 각종 재료 및 양념을 넣어 즉석에서 만들어주는 샐러드

(2) 혼합 샐러드(Combined Salad)
과일 샐러드 : 야채에 과일이 혼합된 샐러드

생선 샐러드 : 야채에 생선이 혼합된 샐러드, 참치 샐러드, 게살 샐러드, 오징어 샐러드

육류 샐러드 : 야채와 육류가 혼합된 샐러드, 소고기 샐러드 등

• 셰프 샐러드 : 양상추, 햄, 치즈, 닭고기, 계란, 토마토, 올리브 등을 이용해 만든 주방장 특선 샐러드

2) Dressing (드레싱)

샐러드와 함께 서빙하는 소스를 일컫는 말. 미국에서는 드레싱이란 표현을 쓰는데, 유럽에서는 그냥 소스라고 한다. 우리나라에서는 드레싱과 소스를 모두 사용한다.

드레싱이란 말은 본래 몸단장을 마무리한다는 뜻, 소스를 샐러드 위에 뿌리면 여자가 옷으로 치장하는 것처럼 여겨지는 데서 유래. 드레싱은 샐러드의 맛을 한층 높여주고, 시각적인 면에서 돋보이게 한다. 샐러드 위에 뿌리는 드레싱은 약간 흘러 내려야 정상이다.

드레싱의 종류

(1) 사우전드 아일랜드 드레싱(Thousand Island Dressing)

일명 '천 개의 섬 드레싱'이라고 불림. 마요네즈에 칠리소스, 토마토 케첩, 계란, 양파, 피망, 피클 등을 혼합하여 만듦.

(2) 프렌치 드레싱(French Dressing)

식용유, 식초, 소금, 후추에 양파, 파슬리, 피망 등을 다져 넣고 겨자와 향료를 가미하여 만들어 향이 강하다

(3) 이탈리안 드레싱(Italian Dressing)

적포도주, 레몬즙, 올리브유, 소금, 후추, 향료 등을 넣어 만든다.

3. Review Exercises

1) Put the following into Korean.

definition	vinegar
acid	seasoning
dressed	occidental
emulsion	starch
thickener	expert
adhere	tear
bruise	

2) Put the following into Korean.

1. We usually think of a salad as a cold dish of greens or other vegetables dressed with oil and vinegar.

2. French dressing is one of the simplest and most widely used of dressings.

3. It consists of oil and vinegar or other acid liquids such as lemon juice or fruit juice, plus seasonings.

4. Mayonnaise is also one of the basic dressings, popular over the occidental worlds.

5. It is an emulsion of eggs, vinegar or lemon juice, oil and seasonings.

6. Of dressings boiled or cooked salad dressing is the only one which is thickened with a starch.

4. English for Fun

1) Grammar Rap 🎧

Shopping

Shopping Shopping
Shopping Shopping
Shopping Shopping
Shopping

We need a loaf of bread
And a jar of jam.
A box of cookies
And a pound of ham.

A bottle of ketchup
A pound of cheese.
A dozen eggs,
And a can of peas.

A head of lettuce,
Half a pound of rice,
A bunch of bananas,
And a bag of ice.
Shopping Shopping
Shopping Shopping
Shopping Shopping
Shopping Shopping

2) Exercise about Seasoning (양념)

Seasoning, Seasoning!

다음 양념들을 보기에서 찾아 영어로 적어 보시오.

soybean sauce, salt, mustard, ginger,
sugar, sesame oil, garlic, pepper, vinegar

1. 설탕

2. 생강

3. 겨자

4. 마늘

5. 간장

6. 소금

7. 참기름

8. 식초

9. 후추

Part 2 — Culinary English

1. Recipe Reading & Writing Exercise (레시피 연습)

• Banana Bread Recipe

Match the correct word to each picture.

Verbs	pour stir mix
Nouns	loaf pan bowl wire rack

Read the directions below for making Banana Bread.

1. Preheat oven to 350°F.

2. Lightly grease a 9×5 loaf pan.

3. In a big bowl, mix flour, soda and salt.

4. In another bowl, mix together butter and brown sugar.

5. Stir in eggs and mashed bananas.

6. Stir banana mix into flour mix.

7. Pour mix into loaf pan.

8. Bake in preheated oven for 60-65 minutes.

9. Let bread cool in pan for 10 minutes, then turn out onto a wire rack.

What are the ingredients?

1.

2.

3.

4.

5.

6.

7.

8.

2. Kitchen Equipment (주방 장비) **(1)**

1) Preparatory Equipment (준비용 장비)

(1) Scale(저울)

계량 및 측정용 도구로서 아날로그 저울과 디지털 저울이 있다.

| 아날로그 저울 | 디지털 저울 | 스탠드형 디지털 저울 |

(2) Work Table(작업대)

스테인리스 스틸(Stainless Steel) 강판으로 제작, 표준화된 규격을 사용한다. 가장 간단한 작업대부터 시작하여 밑에 캐비닛(Cabinet)이 있는 작업대, 이동용 작업대, 밑에 선반이 부착된 작업대 등이 있다.

(3) Steam Table(Hot Table, 증기 테이블)

요리작업대의 앞뒤에 배치, 일정한 따뜻한 온도를 유지시키며, 각종 소스 수프 등을 따뜻이 보관하여 고객에게 서비스할 수 있게 하는 테이블이다.

(4) Cold Table(Sandwich Table, Cold Cabinet, 냉장 테이블)

요리 작업대 겸 냉장 기능을 병행하는 테이블, 재료를 차갑게 유지시키며, 주로 전채요리, 후식, 차가운 소스, 과일, 채소 등을 고객에게 차갑게 서비스할 수 있도록 하는 테이블이다.

(5) Sink Unit(싱크대)

싱크대는 반드시 배관과 연결되어야 한다. 개수구의 숫자에 따라서 1구, 2구, 3구 등이 있다.

2) Cooling and Storage Equipment (냉각 및 저장 장비)

(1) Refrigerator(Stand Type)(냉장고)

재료를 차게 보관하는 냉장고. 규격화되어 있으며 독립된 공간의 칸막이로 재료를 분리하며 보통 영상 4~6℃에서 보관한다.

(2) Freezer(냉동고)

재료를 장기간 냉동하는 냉동고. 보통 −10℃ 이하로 보관하며 생선이나 갑각류의 경우, −20℃ 이하에서 보관한다.

(3) Work Table & Cold Table(작업대 겸용 냉장고)

작업대를 겸한 냉장고로 바닥에 낮게 설치. 공간 효율성을 위해 하부는 냉장고로 상부는 작업대로 활용한다.

(4) Showcase

냉장고를 외부에서 투시가 가능하도록 한 것으로 주방에서는 신선 야채, 소스, 드레싱 및 치즈 등을 보관한다.

(5) Ice Cube Maker

가루 얼음(Flake)을 만들 때 사용하는 기계로 주로 식당에서 음료수를 냉각하는 데 많이 이용한다.

3) Washing Equipment (세척용 장비)

(1) Dish Washer(Dish Washing Machine)(식기세척기)

예비 세척(Pre rinse) → 본 세척 및 열풍 건조(Heat Drying)의 순서로 작동하며 다음 세가지 형태가 있다.

a. Conveyor Type (컨베이어형)

긴 체인이나 벨트에 의하여 회전하며 나온다. 단체급식을 주로 하는 대형식당, 공장 및 병원 등의 주방에서 많이 이용한다.

b. Rack Type (선반형)

컨베이어형보다는 보다 작은 용량으로 대형 레스토랑, 호텔 단위주방에서 많이 사용된다.

c. Door Type (도어형)

제일 작은 소형으로 간이 식당, 카페 등에서 이용된다.

3. Cuisine Quiz (조리 퀴즈)

1. Name the three basic salad dressings.

2. What are the two principal ingredients in French dressing?

UNIT 9 Soups

Part 1 · English Skill Up

1. Vocabulary Preview
2. Reading
3. Review Exercises
4. English for Fun

Part 2 · Culinary English

1. Recipe Reading & Writing Exercise(레시피 연습)
2. Kitchen Equipment(주방 장비)(2)
3. Cuisine Quiz(조리 퀴즈)

Part 1   English Skill Up

1. Vocabulary Preview 🎧

liquid	액체
depending on(upon)~	~에 따라
classify	분류하다
principal	기본적인
thickness	뻑뻑한 정도
ingredient	성분
stock/ broth	고기 국물
classification	분류
shellfish	조개
sieve	체

2. Reading 🎧

SOUPS

1) Soups are liquids which can be very thin or quite thick depending upon what they contain.

    ① thick soup

    ② clear soup

    ③ light soup

    ④ heavy soup

2) They are classified according to their thickness or to the principal liquid or other ingredients they contain. Here is one system of classification

① Stocks or broths

② Cream soup : those thickened with a thin veloute, bechamel or white sauce.

③ Bisque : heavy cream soups containing shellfish.

④ Puree : thickened with cooked vegetables or fish passed through a sieve.

⑤ Chowder : thick soup or stew usually containing seafood, potatoes, and milk or cream.

⑥ Potage or Paysanne : broths heavy with ingredients, such as gumbo, chicken noodle or vegetable

• Reading Helper

1. 수프(Soup)는 액체, 함유물에 따라 맑은 수프, 진한 수프로 분류

2. 수프의 구분 : 액체의 주요성분, 농도, 기타 식재료에 따라 분류

기본적인 분류체계

❶ Stocks or broths : 고기 국물

❷ Cream soup : 크림 수프, veloute, bechamel, white sauce를 넣어 진하게 한 것

❸ Bisque : 비스크, 조개를 넣어 만든 걸쭉한 수프

❹ Puree : 퓌레, 익은 야채 또는 체(sieve)로 걸러낸 생선을 넣은 진한 액체

❺ Chowder : 차우더, 해산물, 감자, 우유를 함유한 진한 수프, 또는 스튜

❻ Potage or Paysanne : 포타주, 페이잔느, 오크라, 치킨누들, 야채 등을 넣은 진한 국물(broth)

• More about Soup

1) 흔히 말하는 수프의 두 종류 : 포타주 (Potage)와 콩소메 (consommé)

진한 수프를 포타주, 맑은 수프를 콩소메로 구분한다. 콩소메는 포타주 클레르 (Potage Clair)라고 해서 맑은 수프를 말한다. 진한 수프는 야채수프, 크림수프 등으로 콩소메보다 섬세한 맛은 덜하나 감자, 옥수수, 야채 등의 내용을 첨가해 맛이 더 진하다. 포타주 수프의 경우에는 담백한 요리가 어울리고, 콩소메의 경우는 진한 맛의 요리가 어울리며 코스가 많은 정찬 요리에 적합하다.

2) 수프의 종류

- 온도에 따른 분류 : Hot Soup, Cold Soup
- 농도에 따른 분류 : Clear Soup, Thick Soup

3) 국물이 맑은 수프 (Clear Soup)

① 콩소메(Consommé) : Stock에 쇠고기와 야채를 넣어 끓인 다음 기름을 걸러내어 맑게 한 수프. 맛이 담백하고 깔끔하며 시원하다.

② 부용(Bouillon) : Stock에 육류, 야채, 허브를 함께 삶아 풍미가 우러나며 걸러서 만든 맑고 향기로운 수프. 허브향이 후각을 자극한다.

4) 국물이 진한 수프(Thick Soup)

① 크림수프(Cream Soup)

밀가루를 버터에 볶은 루(Roux)에 생크림과 계란 노른자로 마무리하여 만든 수프. 주재료에 따라 양송이 크림수프, 바닷가재 크림수프, 단호박 크림수프 등이 있다.

② 퓌레(Puree)

당근, 감자, 옥수수, 호박 등의 야채를 바짝 졸인 후 체에 걸러내어 묽게 만든 야채수프로 은은한 향이 일품이다.

③ 차우더(Chowder)

육류, 어패류, 채소류 등을 큼직하게 썰어 넣고 건더기를 많게 한 수프이며, 우유나 크림을 넣어 맛을 부드럽게 하고 그윽한 향기를 깊게 한다. 불어로는 비스크(Bisque)라고도 한다.

5) 세계 각국의 유명한 수프

① 미네스트론 수프(Minestrone Soup)

이태리 야채수프, 여러가지 야채와 스파게티면, 베이컨, 마늘 등으로 만들어 향이 강하고 국물이 진함. 얼큰하고 자극적인 맛, 특유의 향신료 향이 특색임.

② 어니언 수프(Onion Soup)

남프랑스의 대표적 수프로서, 콩소메, 양파, 치즈를 주재료로 함. 양파 향이 강하며 치즈의 맛을 함께 느끼도록 함. 수프가 담겨 나오는 볼이 뜨거우므로 주의.

③ 클램 차우더 수프(Clam Chowder Soup)

미국의 대표적 수프. 대합을 주재료로 하며 시원한 국물 맛이 일품이다.

3. Review Exercises

1) Put the following into Korean.

liquid	depending on(upon)
classify	principal
thickness	ingredient
stock/broth	classification
shellfish	sieve

2) Put the following into Korean.

1. Soups are liquids which can be very thin or quite thick depending upon what they contain.

2. They are classified according to their thickness or to the principal liquid or other ingredients they contain.

3. Bisque is a heavy cream soup containing shellfish.

4. Puree is thickened with cooked vegetables or fish passed through a sieve.

5. Chowder is a thick soup or stew usually containing seafood, potatoes, and milk or cream.

6. Potage or paysanne are broths heavy with ingredients, such as gumbo, chicken noodle or vegetable.

4. English for Fun

• Grammar Rap 🎧

How Much Salt Should I Put in the Soup?

How much salt should I put in the soup?
    Just a little, not too much.
How many onions should I put in the salad?
    Just a few, not too many.

How much pepper should I put in the stew?
    Just a little, not too much.
How many eggs should I put in the omelette?
    Just a few, not too many.

Salt in the soup,
    Pepper in the stew,
Eggs in the omelette,
    Just a few.

Just a little, not too much.
Not too many, just a few.
Just a few, not too many.
Not too many. Just one or two.

8. some butter / Use / for cooking.

9. the pancakes / cook / Finally / in a frying pan.

3. Kitchen Equipment (주방 장비)(2)

1) Processing Equipment (가공용 장비)

재료를 요리 직전에 원하는 형태로 미리 가공할 때 사용하는 장비. 작업을 세분화하고, 작업시간을 단축시켜 능률을 올린다.

(1) Food Slicer(Slicing Machine)(식재료 절단기)

각종 재료를 얇게 썰 수 있는 기기. 고기를 써는 것(Meat Slicer)과 야채를 써는 것(Vegetable Slicer)으로 분류된다.

(2) Food Cutter Mixer(식재료 커터믹서기)

분쇄된 재료를 믹싱(Mixing)하는 기계로 혼합반죽을 만들 때 사용한다.

(3) Meat Grinder(Mincer)(고기 그라인더)

덩어리 재료를 넣어서 잘고 가늘게 분쇄하는 기계로 흔히 정육점에서 볼 수 있다. 육류(소, 돼지고기 및 닭 등) 및 생선류를 잘게 간다. 그라인딩(Grinding)과 민싱(Mincing)은 거의 같은 방법이다.

(4) Cutter Mixer(커터믹서기)

소시지 반죽, 어묵 등의 가공용 육제품을 만들 때 사용하는 혼합반죽기. 갈은 고기에 갖은 양념(Condiment) 및 스파이스(Spice)를 넣고 골고루 반죽하는 기계이다.

(5) Vacuum Packer(Vacuum Packing Machine)(진공포장기)

만든 제품을 진공 포장할 때 사용하는 기계로 제품의 장기보관 및 변색 및 탈색을 방지하고 풍미를 지속적으로 보관하는 데 도움을 준다.

(6) Sausage Stuffer(소시지 스터퍼)

소시지를 만들 때 혼합반죽을 원통형에 넣어 필요한 형상을 만드는 기계. 비엔나 소시지, 프랑크푸르트 소시지 등 색상 및 모양에 따라서 여러 종류의 소시지를 생산한다.

(7) Smoking Box(훈연 박스)

훈제(훈연)할 필요가 있을 때 사용하는 장비로 냉훈법 및 온훈법이 사용된다.

(8) Meat Tenderizer(고기 연화기)

고기를 부드럽게 하기 위하여 칼집을 내는 기계를 말한다.

Meat Slicer   Vegetable Slicer   Cutter Mixer   Meat Grinder

Meat Grinder   Broiler   Griddle

2) Heat Source Equipment (열원장비)

전기, 가스, 스팀을 이용하여 요리를 하는 장비. 내부는 고열이기 때문에 항상 안전에 유의해야 한다.

(1) Gas Range with Oven(가스 오븐 레인지)

주방에서 이용하는 가장 기본적이고 중요한 조리기기이다. 윗부분은 레인지가 설치되어 있어 각종 프라이팬을 이용한 조리를 할 수 있고, 아랫부분은 오븐이 설치되어 로우스팅(Roasting) 요리를 할 수 있는 다목적 오븐이다.

(2) Induction Range(인덕션 레인지)

전기를 사용하여 금속플레이트(Plate)를 가열하여 이용하는 레인지.

(3) Broiler(브로일러, 석쇠, 직화구이)

스테이크나 생선 및 갑각류를 직화(직접열)로 굽는 기계이다.

(4) Salamander Broiler(salamander, 도롱뇽 브로일러)

일반 가열 조리기기와는 달리 불꽃이 위에서 아래로 내려오는 하향식 열 기기로, 각종 그라탕(Gratin) 요리에 이용된다. 가스식이 주종을 이루며 직화요리에는 필수적이다.

(5) Griddle(그리들)

두께 10mm 정도의 철판으로 만들어진 조리기기. 아침식사 시의 계란 요리, 볶음밥, 팬케이크(Pan Cake), 핫 샌드위치(Hot Sandwich) 등 조리의 범위가 다양하다.

(6) Steam Cooker(Steamer)(찜기)

고열의 증기를 이용하여 식품을 조리하는 기기. 밥을 짓거나 찜 요리를 하는 데 이용할 수 있다. 고압, 고열의 증기를 사용하므로 기기의 개폐 시 증기에 의한 화상에 주의한다.

(7) Steam Kettle(Tilting)(기울어지는 증기솥 혹은 주전자)

고열의 증기를 이용한 조리 기기. Soup이나 Sauce를 대량으로 생산하는 데 이용된다.

(8) Fryer(Deep Fat)(튀김기)

각종 튀김요리를 하는 데 이용되는 기기. 고열에 의한 기름의 산화를 방지하기 위하여 온도를 적정선으로 유지하여야 하며 튀기지 않을 때에는 전원을 완전히 끄지 않고 대기 상태에 두어 언제나 요리가 가능하도록 한다.

(9) Oven(오븐)
① **Convection Oven**(컨벡션 오븐, 대류식 오븐)

오븐 내부에 팬을 설치, 열풍의 대류를 이용. 전기로 뜨거운 열을 이용하여 요리하는 오븐. 전기식과 가스식이 있다.

② **Reel Oven**(릴 오븐)

오븐 내부에 체인을 이용한 트레이(Tray)를 설치하여 팬을 얹을 수 있게 한 오븐. 중형 생산 공장에 주로 사용되며 대량생산의 터널 오븐과 로터리 오븐의 중간형이다.

③ **Pizza Oven**(피자 오븐)

고열을 순간적으로 발생시켜 피자 및 파이를 전용으로 굽는 오븐. 레스토랑 및 카페 등에서 많이 이용한다.

④ **Deck Oven**(데크 오븐)

선반 형태의 서랍식 오븐으로 현재 제과, 제빵에서 가장 보편적으로 사용되는 오븐이며 가스, 전기식이 있다. 일반적인 빵류와 케이크류, 페스트리류까지 광범위하게 쓰임.

⑤ **Rotary Oven**(로터리 오븐, 렉오븐)

내부에 선반(rack)이 있어서 좌우 혹은 상하로 회전하며 굽는 오븐으로 비교적 대용량의 제품생산에 적합한 오븐이다.

⑥ **Tunnel Oven**(터널 오븐)

오븐에 체인(Chain)이나 벨트(Belt)를 설치하여 컨베이어 라인을 연결하여 균일한 온도로 생산하는 고용량의 오븐이다.

⑦ **Microwave Oven**(전자레인지)

초단파를 이용한 오븐으로 간단하게 해동시키거나 데울 때 많이 사용한다.

3) Baking Equipment (제과용 장비)

각종 빵이나 케이크용 반죽을 만들고 발효를 시키고 굽는 모든 장비이다.

(1) Mixer(믹서)

빵, 케이크 및 쿠키를 만드는 데 필요한 반죽을 만들 수 있는 기계이다. 모양 및 용도에 따라서 다음과 같이 세분화된다.

① **Table Type Mixer**(테이블형 믹서)

소형 혼합기로서 탁상이나 테이블 위에 올려 놓고 소량의 식재료를 믹싱하거나 거품을 내는 데 이용되며, 이동이 쉽고 무게가 가벼워 적은 양의 반죽 만들기에 적합하다.

② **Bench Type Mixer**(벤치타입 믹서)

대형 믹서로서 바닥에 수평으로 설치하여 반죽을 만드는 데 사용한다.

③ **Spiral Mixer**(나선형 믹서)

나선형 훅이 내장되어 있어 프랑스빵(French Bread)이나 토스트 브레드(Toast Bread) 같은 반죽이나 글루텐 형성 능력이 떨어지는 밀가루로 빵을 만들 때 적합하다.

(2) Proofer(발효기)

반죽을 발효시키는 발효기로서 온도와 습도를 적정하게 유지해야 한다.

(3) Dough Sheeter(반죽 펼치기)

처진 반죽을 편평하게 펴는 '다리미' 같은 역할을 한다. 롤러(Roller)의 간격 조절로 반죽의 두께를 조절하며 밀어 펼 수 있는 기계. 페스트리(Pastry) 반죽을 만들 때 많이 사용한다.

(4) Dough Divider(Pastry roller)(반죽분할기)

반죽을 분할하여 둥글게 해주는 기기. 소프트롤(Soft Roll), 하드롤(Hard Roll) 등의 롤 종류를 분할 및 둥글리기할 때에 사용된다.

(5) French Bread Moulder(프랑스빵 몰더, 긴빵 성형기)

일정한 양의 반죽을 분할해 기계에 넣고 조작하면 원하는 길이와 굵기로 말아주는 기기. 길이가 긴 빵에 사용된다.

(6) Ice Cream Machine(Maker)(아이스크림 믹서)

아이스크림의 제조방법에 따라 식재료를 계량하여 살균, 소독 탱크에 넣고 냉각시킨 후에 회전냉각 거품기포 장치에 넣고 작동시키면 아이스크림이 제조되는 설비

(7) Oven(오븐)

나무, 전기, 가스 등을 이용하여 빵을 굽는 기기

4) Coffee Making Equipment (커피용 장비)

(1) Coffee Machine

① **Coffee Urn**(주둥이가 달린 커피포트)

대형 커피 추출기로부터 커피 분말을 필터 (Filter)에 넣고 버튼을 누르면 뜨거운 물이 필터 속 커피에 떨어져서 추출되는 커피 기기. 대규모 연회 시에 많은 고객에게 동시에 제공할 수 있도록 대용량으로 설계되어 있다.

② **Coffer Brewer**

중소형 커피추출기로 연회나 레스토랑에서 고객을 위해 사용하는 중형 커피추출기이다.

③ **Coffee Machine**(Automatic)

커피 원두의 분쇄에서 추출까지 원터 치(One Touch)로 작동되는 자동식 커 피 기기. 컴퓨터 회로가 내장되어 있다. 고객이 주문하는 커피를 취향에 따라 제 공하며 레스토랑, 커피전문점 등에 많이

설치된다. 자동화된 기기이기 때문에 충격을 주거나 수분이 침투되지 않도록 각별히 유의해야 한다.

(2) Juice Dispenser(주스 냉각기)

각종 주스류를 차갑게 보관하는 기기. 주로 뷔페에서 많이 사용

(3) Waffle Baker(와플제조기)

Breakfast에 제공되는 와플(Waffle)을 굽는 조리 기기

(4) Toaster

대량으로 토스트를 구울 수 있도록 설계된 회전식 기기. Coffee Shop 또는 Room Service 주방에서 많이 사용된다.

4. Cuisine Quiz (조리 퀴즈)

1. What kind of soup would logically be served with a heavy meal? (light / heavy)

2. A consommé(콩소메) is a (clear / thick) soup.

3. A bisque is a heavy cream soup which includes

      .

4. A potage or paysanne soup is a (heavy / light) soup.

UNIT 10 Seafoods

Part 1 · English Skill Up

1. Vocabulary Preview
2. Reading
3. Review Exercises
4. English for Fun

Part 2 · Culinary English

1. Recipe Reading & Writing Exercise(레시피 연습)
2. Cuisine Quiz(조리 퀴즈)

1. Vocabulary Preview 🎧

poultry	가금류	tenderness	부드러움
flesh	살, 고기	closely	밀접하게
related	관련 있는	dictate	지시하다
shellfish	조개	lean	지방이 적은
fat	지방이 많은	deteriorate	부패하다
deterioration	부패	bacterial	박테리아의
flavor	풍미, 맛	ammonia	암모니아
odor	냄새	storage	저장
shrimp	새우	clam	대합
crab	게	lobster	바닷가재
oyster	굴	abalone	전복

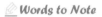 *Words to Note*

oyster	crab	clam	lobster
굴	게	대합	바닷가재

2. Reading 🎧

SEAFOODS

1) We decide how to cook meat or poultry largely on the basis of the tenderness of the flesh, which is closely related to age.

2) With fish, the fat content dictates the cooking method.
   ① Shellfish (Lean fish): low in fat - poached, deep fried, or baked in a sauce.
   ② Fat fish: broiled, baked or pan fried.

3) Seafood deteriorates much more quickly than most meats. Bacterial growth is faster and flavor falls off quickly. A sharp ammonia odor or fishy smell means deterioration.

The Storage Life
   ① Top quality fresh fish - 5 days
   ② Shrimp - 7 days
   ③ Live clam, crab, lobster - 14 days
   ④ Oysters in the shell - 20 days

• Summary

1. 육류, 가금류 조리방법: 육질의 연함 정도에 따라 결정, 연령과 밀접한 관련

2. 생선의 조리법: 함유한 fat에 따라 결정

   ① 지방이 적은(Lean fish), 갑각류: poaching, deep frying, baking에 적합

   ② 지방이 많은(Fat fish): broiling, pan frying, baking에 적합

3. 해산물은 육류보다 빨리 부패, 박테리아 번식이 빠르며 맛이 떨어짐

4. 저장기간

   ① 최상의 신선한 생선 – 5일

   ② 새우 – 7일

   ③ 살아 있는 대합, 게, 바닷가재 – 14일

   ④ 껍질 속의 굴 – 20일

• More about Fish

생선요리는 수프 다음에 제공되는 코스 음식에 해당되나, 육류를 대체하는 주요리 역할도 한다. 육류를 기피하는 손님들이 선호하는 요리가 되었다. 지방성분이 적고 비타민과 칼슘이 풍부하므로 건강식, 담백하고 소화가 잘 된다. 생선요리 대신에 파스타(Pasta)가 제공되기도 한다.

1) 생선요리의 종류

① 바다생선(Fish) : 대구(Cod), 청어(Herring), 도미(Sea Bream), 농어(Sea Bass), 참치(Tuna), 넙치(Halibut), 혀가자미(Sole) 등

② 조개류(Shellfish) : 전복(Abalone), 홍합(Mussel), 가리비(Scallop), 대합(Clam), 굴(Oyster) 등

③ 갑각류(Crustacea) : 왕새우(Prawn), 바닷가재(Lobster), 게(Crab), 새우

(Shrimp) 등

④ 연체류(Mollusca) : 오징어(Cuttle Fish), 문어(Octopus) 등

⑤ 민물생선(Fresh Water Fish) : 송어(Trout), 연어(Salmon), 은어(Sweet Fish) 등

2) 레몬과 생선요리

생선요리에는 비린 냄새를 없애기 위하여 레몬을 제공한다. 레몬을 짜는 방법은 레몬의 한쪽 끝을 포크로 고정시키고 나이프로 가볍게 눌러 즙을 낸다. 생선프라이나 석쇠구이

등의 요리에는 하프 레몬이 곁들어진다. 이때는 오른손의 엄지, 중지, 집게손가락으로 즙을 내어 생선 위에 뿌린다. 이때 레몬 스퀴저(Lemon Squeezer)를 사용하면 레몬을 손쉽게 짤 수 있다. 즙이 튀지 않도록 왼손으로 가리면서 짜면 안전하게 잘 짤 수 있다.

3. Review Exercises

1) Put the following into Korean.

poultry	tenderness
flesh	closely
related	dictate
shellfish	lean
fat	deteriorate
deterioration	bacterial
flavor	ammonia
odor	storage
shrimp	clam
crab	lobster
oyster	

2) Put the following into Korean.

1. With fish, the fat content dictates the cooking method.

2. Shellfish (Lean fish) is low in fat - poached, deep fried, or baked in a sauce.

3. Fat fish is broiled, baked or pan fried.

4. Seafood deteriorates much more quickly than most meats.

5. Bacterial growth is faster and flavor falls off quickly.

6. A sharp ammonia odor or fishy smell means deterioration.

4. English for Fun

Grammar Tips

① How Much? How Many?

② Not Too Much, Just a Little.

Dialogue 1 🎧

Mother	How much milk do you want?
Daughter	Not too much. Just a little.
Mother	Okay. Here you are.
Daughter	Thanks.
Roommate1	How many cookies do you want?
Roommate2	Not too many. Just a few.

| Roommate1 | Okay. Here you are. |
| Roommate2 | Thanks. |

Dialogue 2 🎧

Nancy	Would you like some coffee?
Maria	Yes, please. Just a little.
Nancy	Is that too much?
Maria	No, That's fine. Thank.
Nancy	Do you add milk in your coffee?
Maria	Yes, please. But not too much.
	That's fine.
Nancy	Sugar?
Maria	Just a little, please.
Nancy	So what's new with you?
Maria	Not too much. How about you?
Nancy	Oh, not too much.

Part 2   Culinary English

1. Recipe Reading & Writing Exercise (레시피 연습)

• Fudge Brownies

Ingredients

12 ounces	best-quality chocolate
¾ cup	butter
1 ¼ cups	sugar
1 tablespoon	vanilla
4 large	eggs
1 teaspoon	salt
1 cup	all-purpose flour
1 cup	chocolate chips
1 cup	walnuts, chopped

* Fill the blank with the right verb.

cool, stir, preheat, pour, melt, bake, grease, place

Directions

1. oven to 350F and   rack in middle of oven.

2. 13" × 9" baking pan.

3. _____ chocolate with butter, stirring, until mixture is smooth.

4. Let _____ until lukewarm.

5. _____ in sugar, vanilla and eggs, one at a time, stirring well after each addition.

6. _____ in salt and flour, stirring just until combined.

7. _____ in chocolate chips and walnuts.

8. _____ into prepared baking pan and _____ for 25-30 minutes

9. Let _____ completely.

Solutions

1. _Preheat_ oven to 350F and place rack in middle of oven.

2. _Grease_ 13" × 9" baking pan.

3. _Melt_ chocolate with butter, stirring, until mixture is smooth.

4. Let _cool_ until lukewarm.

5. _Stir_ in sugar, vanilla and eggs, one at a time, stirring well after each addition.

6. _Stir_ in salt and flour, stirring just until combined.

7. _Stir_ in chocolate chips and walnuts.

8. _Pour_ into prepared baking pan and _bake_ for 25-30 minutes

9. Let _cool_ completely.

2. Cuisine Quiz(조리 퀴즈)

1. What temperature should be used for holding frozen fish?

2. All shellfish are fat/lean.

3. When a fish smells "fishy" it is ⬛⬛⬛⬛⬛⬛⬛⬛⬛⬛ .

UNIT 11 Bread

Part 1 · English Skill Up

1. Vocabulary Preview
2. Reading
3. Review Exercises
4. English for Fun

Part 2 · Culinary English

1. Recipe Reading & Writing Exercise(레시피 연습)
2. Cooking Method(조리법)
3. Cuisine Quiz(조리 퀴즈)

Part 1 — English Skill Up

1. Vocabulary Preview 🎧

mixture	혼합물	leavening agent	발효 매개물
expand	팽창하다	carbon dioxide	이산화탄소
batter	묽은 반죽	paste	중간 반죽
dough	진한 반죽	knead	반죽하다, 주무르다, 개다
manually	손으로	machinery	기계로
tender	부드러운	shorten	줄이다
gluten	글루텐, 단백질	strand	섬유 가닥
surround	주위를 둘러싸다		

📝 *Words to Note*

- 글루텐 : 곡류 속에 들어있는 저장 단백질, 글리아신 + 글루테닌의 화합물, 밀가루풀 등에서 접착제 역할을 하는 접착성 물질.

- **leavening agent** : 발효매개물, 팽창제

- **shortening** : 쇼트닝, 글루텐 가닥 생성을 단축시킴. 버터, 라드, 식용유, 마가린 등. 시폰 케이크는 식물성 기름으로 함. 상업용 쇼트닝은 버터, 라드, 식용유, 가공쇼트닝, 마가린 등. 빵이나 과자의 조직을 연화시키고 매끄럽게 하여 가소성이 생기게 한다. 쇼트닝 함량이 빵/롤빵은 1~2%, 케이크는 10~20%, 파이 껍질은 30% 이상이다. 함량이 지나치면 케이크가 부풀지 않음. 식물성 기름: 낮은 온도에서도 액체 상태 유지, 딱딱하게 굽는 제품이나 시폰 및 케이크에 사용한다.

2. Reading 🎧

BREAD

1) Baked products are basically wheat flour and milk or water mixtures to which eggs, sugar, shortening and a leavening agent may be added.

2) During baking, the mixtures are expanded by air, steam, and carbon dioxide.

3) Baked products are divided into:

① Batter is beaten during preparation.

- It can be dropped or poured.

※ Ex: cake, muffins, or pancakes.

② Paste is a soft mixture of flour and water with butter and so on.

- It is used in making pastry.

※ Ex: pastry puffs or pie paste.

③ Dough is too thick to be beaten.

- It requires handling or kneading either manually or by machinery.

※ Ex: yeast bread, sweet roll, pastries, and biscuits.

4) Fat or oil used in baking is selected to perform a particular function.

※ Shortening: fats which are used to shorten the gluten strands, to surround them and make them more easily broken. The product is made tenderer.

• Reading Helper

1. Baked Products: (밀가루+물) + (egg, milk, 발효매개물)

2. 밀가루 반죽 부풀게 촉진(공기, 스팀, CO_2)

3. 밀가루 반죽 분류(묽은 정도에 따라)

   ① Batter(가장 묽음) : pour, drop 가능 : cake, muffin, pan cake

   ② Paste(중간 묽음) : 버터 첨가한 밀가루 반죽 : pastry, puff

   ③ Dough(너무 진하여 휘젓지 못함) : 손이나 기계로 처리

4. 특수기능 필요 시: fat 또는 oil 선택

   ① 쇼트닝(shortening) : 밀가루 단백질 섬유가닥(gluten strand)을 짧게 단축시키고, 주위를 감싸 쉽게 부러지게 하며 부드럽게 함.

3. Review Exercises

1) Put the following into Korean.

mixture	leavening agent
expand	carbon dioxide
batter	paste
dough	knead
manually	machinery
tender	shorten
gluten	strand
surround	

2) Put the following into Korean.

1. Baked products are basically wheat flour and milk or water mixtures to which eggs, sugar, shortening and a leavening agent may be added.

2. During baking, the mixtures are expanded by air, steam, and carbon dioxide.

3. Baked products are divided into batter, paste, and dough.

4. Batter is beaten during preparation. It can be dropped or poured.

5. Paste is a soft mixture of flour and water with butter and so on. It is used in making pastry.

6. Dough is too thick to be beaten. It requires handling or kneading either manually or by machinery.

4. English for Fun

Etiquette English

1) How to ask someone if they want something

When asking someone if they want something say "Would you like..............?"

It is more polite then saying "Do you want something?"

Formal	Would you like a sandwich?		
Informal	Do you want a sandwich?		
Very informal	Sandwich?		
Formal	Yes, please	*or*	No, thank you
Informal	Yes, I'd like some	*or*	No, thanks
Very informal	I'd love one	*or*	No

2) How to accept a cup of coffee and how you would you like it

Would you like a cup of coffee?

Formal	Would you like a coffee?
Informal	Do you want a coffee?

Very informal	Coffee?		
Formal	Yes, please	*or*	No, thank you
Informal	Yes, I'd like some	*or*	No, thanks
Very informal	I'd love one	*or*	No

3) Saying how you would like your coffee

Black with sugar, please.

White, no sugar, please.

White with sugar, please.

Black, no sugar, please.

A little milk, but no sugar, please.

Part 2 — Culinary English

1. Recipe Reading & Writing Exercise (레시피 연습)

1) Easy Pancakes

Prep Time : 5 Minutes

Cook Time : 10 Minutes

Ready In : 15 Minutes

Servings : 4

Ingredients

1 cup	all-purpose flour
2 tablespoons	white sugar
2 teaspoons	baking powder
1 teaspoon	salt
1 egg	beaten
1 cup	milk
2 tablespoons	vegetable oil

Directions

1. In a large bowl,   flour, sugar, baking powder and salt.

2. Make a well in the center, and   in milk, egg and oil.   until smooth.

3. Heat a lightly oiled frying pan over medium high heat.
   the batter onto the griddle, using approximately 1/4 cup for each pancake.

4. Brown on both sides and serve hot.

2) Review of Cooking Verbs

Cooking Verbs

To boil	To grate	To chop	To slice	To grill
To fry	To peel	To bake	To pour	To spread
To mix	To roast	To stir	To steam	To beat
To cook	To carve	To melt	To squeeze	To saute
To sprinkle	To cut	To knead	To sift	To serve

3) Exercises

Choose the right one.

1.   the carrot into small circles.

    a. Stir   b. Chop   c. Drain

2.   the lasagne for 30 minutes in the oven

    a. Boil   b. Bake   c. Mix

3. After ten minutes,   the pasta until there is no water left. Then place the pasta into a large bowl

    a. drain   b. fry   c. boil

4.   the onion and throw away the skin.

    a. Fry   b. Stir   c. Peel

5.   the steak with salt, pepper and lemon.

    a. Season   b. Drain   c. Chop

6.   the onion until it is soft, but not brown.

    a. Pour   b. Fry   c. Bake

7. Constantly   the mixture using a wooden spoon.

    a. fry   b. boil   c. stir

8. When the mixture looks shiny,   it into individual dishes.

   a. pour   b. chop   c. fry

9. When you have finished preparing the vegetables, them together with your hands

   a. pour   b. mix   c. chop

10.   the pasta for ten minutes, or until soft.

   a. Boil   b. Bake   c. Fry

2. Cooking Method (조리법)

1) Different cooked or prepared food

flambé   stir-fry   fry   boil

bake   toast   steam   stew   barbecue

출처 https://www.easypacelearning.com/design/images/waysofcooking.jpg

2) 조리의 종류

(1) Boil(삶다)

Boiling(보일링; 삶기)은 물이나 Stock 속에서 액체를 비등점까지 급속적으로 끓이는 방법이다. 파스타, 밥, 혹은 말린 야채 조리에 주로 사용한다.

(2) Simmer(부글부글 계속 끓이다. 국을 끓이다. 불을 줄여서 계속 끓이는 것)

Simmering(시머링)은 비등점 이하에서 요리하는 방법으로 포칭할 때의 온도보다 높다. 보일링을 하다가 불을 약간 줄여 94℃ 정도로 요리한다.

(3) Steam(찌다)

Steaming(찌기)은 밀폐된 용기 내에서 증기압을 이용해 재료를 찌는 조리 방법이다. 식품 고유의 맛을 유지할 수 있는 건강한 요리법으로 간주된다.

(4) Blanch(데치다)

Blanching(데치기)은 야채나 고기 등을 끓는 물에 짧은 시간 동안 넣었다가 건져 흐르는 찬물에 헹구는 조리방법. 냄새 제거, 조직 연화 및 재료 고유의 색상을 선명하게 하는 역할을 한다. 처음부터 물과 함께 끓일 경우 야채, 고기세포가 열려 맛이 손실될 우려가 있으나, 뜨거운 물에 데칠 경우 세포막이 열리지 않으므로 맛을 보존할 수 있다.

(5) Poach(생선을 졸이다, 수란을 만들다)

Poaching(포칭)은 물, 우유, 육수, 포도주 등의 액체에서 서서히 부드럽게 내용물을 익히는 조리방법이다. 계란 또는 생선 등을 비등점 이하에서 끓이는 방법으로 음식이 건조해지거나 딱딱해지는 것을 방지해 준다.

(6) Fry(튀기다)

Frying(튀기기)는 기름 사용 양에 따라 다음 세 가지로 분류된다.

① **Pan-Fry**(얇게 튀기다)

Pan-frying(팬 튀김)은 소량의 기름만 사용하는 것으로 편평한 팬에서 조리하는 형태를 말한다. (군만두, 불고기 등)

② **Stir-Fry**(저으면서 볶다)

Stir-frying(저으면서 볶는 야채볶음)은 중국요리에서 많이 이용하며 팬에서 기름으로 볶으면서 요리하는 방법이다.

③ **Deep-Fry**(깊이 튀기다)

Deep-frying(깊이 튀김)은 식품재료를 기름에 잠기게 하여, 조리 중 기름 온도가 강하하지 않도록 식품량을 적당하게 조절하며 튀기는 요리법이다. 기름 온도가 너무 낮으면 재료가 기름을 흡수한다.

(7) Gratin(그라탕)

Gratin(그라탕)은 마무리 요리방법으로 크림, 치즈, 계란 및 버터 등을 요리 위에 놓고 열을 이용하여 표면을 갈색화하는 요리법이다. 프랑스 요리에서 시작되었다. 예) Gratin Pizza

(8) Braise(고기를 굽다)

Braising(브레이징)은 습식열(moist heat) 및 건식열(dry heat)을 동시에 이용하는데, 고온에서 재료를 그슬린 다음 적정량의 액체를 넣고 Pot에서 뚜껑을 덮고 요리하는 방법이다.

(9) Bake(굽다)

Baking(굽기)은 오븐에서 건식열(dry heat)을 이용하여 요리하는 방법이다.

(10) Grill or Broil(석쇠에 굽다, 오븐 열선에서 센 불로 바로 익히다)

Grilling(or Broiling)(그릴링 혹은 브로일링)은 식품의 표면에 건식열을 이용하여 요리하는 방법으로 그릴(석쇠)이나 그리들(번철)을 이용하며 직접 열로 하기 때문에 바비큐나 구이에 적합하다. 특히 숯(Charcoal)을 사용할 경우 음식에 특유한 맛을 더한  다. 고기 두께가 얇을수록 온도는 높아야 하며 두꺼울수록 온도는 낮아야 한다. 그릴링은 가열된 금속의 표면에 대고 굽는 방법으로 간접적으로 익히는 방법이고, 브로일링은 석쇠 위에 얹어 불꽃에 직접 닿게 하여 굽는 방법이다.

(11) Roast(굽다)

Roasting(로스팅)은 건식열(dry heat)을 이용하며, 화염이나 오븐을 사용해 기름을 계속 칠하면서 굽는 방법이다. 소고기, 닭, 칠면조, 양다리 구이 등에 사용하며, 덩어리째 굽는데 재료의 표면에 있는 지방질이 녹아 고기 내부로 스며들어 맛을 더해준다.

(12) Smoke(훈제하다)

Smoking(훈제)은 연기(smok)를 사용하여 독특한 향(flavor)과 저장성을 더해주는 방법으로 햄(ham), 소시지(sausage), 베이컨(bacon) 과 훈제연어(smoked salmon) 등 생선류에 사용된다.

(13) Stew(스튜, 죽으로 끓이다)

Stewing(뭉근히 끓이기)는 팬이나 냄비를 이용하여 낮은 온도로 서서히 조리는 방법으로 Meats, Vegetables에 사용하는 조리법이다. 고기나 야채 등을 큼직하게 썰어 기름에 볶은 후 육수를 넣어 걸쭉하게 끓이는 방법으로 우리나라의 갈비찜과 같은 조리법이다.

(14) Glaze(글레이즈, 설탕 시럽 등을 바르다)

Glazing(글레이징)은 표면에 코팅을 입히는 요리법으로 설탕, 버터 물 또는 육수(stock)를 야채에 첨가한 다음 뚜껑을 덮고 약한 불에서 서서히 졸이는 것이다. 물기가 거의 증발한 다음 뚜껑(lid 혹은 cover)을 열고 계속 흔들어 준다. 당근이나 무 등에 적합하다. 예) glazed doughnut

(15) Whip(거품내다, 채찍질하듯 치다)

Whipping(휘핑, 거품내기)은 거품기(whipper)나 포크를 사용하여 빠른 속도로 거품을 내고 공기를 함유하게 하는 방법으로 계란 흰자(egg white) 또는 휘핑크림(whipping Cream)의 거품을 낼 때 쓰는 방법이다.

(16) Blend(혼합하다)

Blending(브렌딩, 혼합)은 두 가지 이상의 식재료들이 잘 혼합될 수 있도록 믹서기(blender)를 이용하여 믹스(mixing)하는 방법이다.

3. Cuisine Quiz (조리 퀴즈)

1. The principal gas formed by growing Yeast is   .

2. Custard pies are baked at (lower/higher) temperatures than fruit pies.

3. In a chiffon cake, what is used in the recipe instead of fat?

4. A Shortening shortens what?

UNIT 12 Roasting

Part 1 · English Skill Up

1. Vocabulary Preview
2. Reading
3. Review Exercises
4. English for Fun

Part 2 · Culinary English

1. Recipe Reading & Writing Exercise(레시피 연습)
2. Kitchen Utensil(조리기구)
3. About Beef
4. Cuisine Quiz(조리 퀴즈)

Part 1 — **English Skill Up**

1. Vocabulary Preview 🎧

method	방법	professional	전문적인, 전문가
rack	선반 걸이	baste	구우면서 육즙을 끼얹다
internal	내부의	thermometer	온도계
Celsius [centigrade] thermometer	섭씨 온도계	Fahrenheit thermometer	화씨 온도계
muscle	근육	tissue	조직
distort	왜곡하다	reliable	신뢰할만한
per pound	파운드 당	weigh	무게 달다
weight	무게	multiply	곱하다
sear	태우다 그슬리다	crust	표피, 껍질
carve	새기다	juicy	육즙이 흐르는
coloration	색 입히기	briefly	간략하게

2. Reading 🎧

ROASTING

Roasting is one of the most common and basic of all cooking methods. You can be a professional cook, too, if you understand and follow the basic rules of roasting.

1) The Basic Rules of Roasting

Use a dry heat only, add no water, and do not cover.

2) Use a rack to keep the roast out of the juices: if cooked without a rack a portion of the meat may stew in the juices at the bottom of the pan.

3) Place the roast fat-side up: The roast will baste in its own juices, and basted by hand as needed.

4) Use an internal thermometer

  ① The professionals can tell by feeling the meat, but until you have an experience with such methods, use an internal thermometer.

  ② Place the point of thermometer in the muscle tissue of the meat, not in fat or against bone, both of which can distort the reading.

  ③ Simply find the internal temperature for the degree of doneness you desire on a reliable meat chart.

5) 300℉ for 20 minutes per pound for rare beef.

  ① As a general rule for determining roasting time, professional, recommend 300℉ for 20 minutes per pound for rare beef.

  ② Simply weigh each item and multiply its weight by 20 minutes.

    Ex: roast weight : 12 pounds 8 ounces

    12.5 pounds × 20 minutes = 250 minutes

6) Searing is not recommended for larger cuts of meat.

① The interior of the seared roast is not uniformly cooked. Searing creates a hard outer crust.

※ The meat that has been cooked at steady low temperature shows no wasteful outside crust, and has uniformly juicy and tasty interior.

② Thin cuts of meat can be seared in order to create an attractive coloration of the surface. They are briefly seared in hot oil or fat, and when the surface is browned, the heat is reduced.

• Reading Helper

1. Roasting 조리법의 기본
   건열만 사용, 물은 불필요, 뚜껑 덮지 않음.

2. 받침대(rack) 사용, roast 고기 덩어리를 받침대 위에 올려놓고 조리하면 팬 바닥에 흘러내리는 육즙과 분리된다.

3. Roast의 지방이 많은 부분이 위가 되게 받침대 위에 올려놓고 조리함

4. 내부 온도계 사용

   ① 전문가는 고기를 느낄 수 있으나 그 경지에 이르기 전에는 내부 온도계 사용

   ② 뾰족한 끝은 근육조직(muscle tissue)에 꽂는다.

   ③ 신뢰성 있는 차트에서 내부 온도 확인

5. Rare beef는 1파운드당 20분 (300℉) 조리함

6. 큰 고깃덩어리는 저열로 서서히 조리, 균일되게 익게 함.

① Searing시킨 roast 내부는 균등하게 요리되지 않고 겉을 딱딱하게 만든다. 낮은 온도로 서서히 익힌 고기는 낭비적인 표면을 만들지 않고 균등하게 육즙이 흐르고 맛있는 속을 만든다.

② 얇은 고기 조각은 표면 색깔이 아름다우려면 고열 oil, fat 속에서 잠시 searing 시킨다.

육류의 다양한 조리방법

- 로스팅(Roasting) : 고깃덩어리를 오븐에 넣어 익혀내는 조리방법

- 브로일링(Broiling) : 석쇠나 팬을 이용하여 굽는 조리방법

- 브레이징(Braising) : 소량의 물을 붓고 약한 불로 장시간 찌는 조리방법

- 그릴링(Grilling) : 고기를 석쇠에 끼워 오븐의 복사열로 짧은 시간에 요리하는 것으로 영양분과 향기의 보존이 가능

- 프라잉(Frying) : 기름으로 튀기는 조리방법

- 소테(Saute) : 버터 또는 오일을 이용하여 굽는 조리방법

- 스튜잉(Stewing) : 고기를 여러 가지 재료와 함께 장시간 약한 불로 졸이는 조리방법

가니쉬(Garnish)란?

육류요리인 스테이크와 함께 제공되는 야채의 종류를 말함. 스테이크는 산성식품이기 때문에 영양학적 균형을 맞추기 위해 알칼리성인 야채를 함께 서비스한다.

가니쉬 제공 목적

① 영양의 균형 맞춤, 산성 스테이크에 알칼리성 야채의 영양학적 균형

② 시각적으로 돋보이기 위함. 적색류(당근, 적색피망 등), 녹색류(브로콜리,

아스파라거스, 녹색피망 등), 흰색류(감자, 무, 파인애플 등)으로 조화 이룸

③ 식욕을 돋구기 위함

3. Review Exercises

1) Put the following into Korean.

method	professional
rack	baste
internal	thermometer
muscle	tissue
distort	reliable
per pound	weigh
weight	multiply
sear	crust
carve	juicy
coloration	briefly

2) Put the following into Korean.

1. Roasting is one of the most common and basic of all cooking methods.

2. The Basic Rules of Roasting: Use a dry heat only, add no water, and do not cover.

3. Use a rack to keep the roast out of the juices.

4. Place the roast fat-side up: The roast will baste in its own juices, and basted by hand as needed.

5. Searing is not recommended for larger cuts of meat.

6. Thin cuts of meat can be seared in order to create an attractive coloration of the surface.

4. English for Fun

1) Grammar Tips: Count Nouns & Noncount Nouns

Fill in the blanks with the words in the list.

> too many,   too much,   they,
> it's,   it(2),   they're(2),   aren't

Interviewer: **What's your favorite food?**

A   My favorite food is cheese. I love cheese. I eat   all the time.

B   I like bananas. I think they're delicious, and   very good for you.

C I like ice cream.   my favorite thing to eat. I have

    ice cream every day.

D My favorite food? Hmm. Let me see. Oh, yes. French fries. I

    love French fries. I know   very good for

    me, but I think they're delicious.

E Coffee, I drink   all the time. Come to think of it, I

    probably drink   coffee, but I really like it.

F I love chocolate chip cookies! I think   great! My

    Mom and Dad say I eat too many, but I say you can never

    eat   chocolate chip cookies. They're

    awesome!

2) Check about Meat

Meat, Meat!

다음 대표적 고기들을 보기에서 찾아 영어로 적어 보시오.

beef, pork, chicken, duck, veal, mutton(lamb), turkey

1. 양고기   2. 칠면조고기

3. 오리고기   4. 송아지고기

5. 쇠고기   6. 돼지고기

7. 닭고기

Part 2 — **Culinary English**

1. Recipe Reading & Writing Exercise (레시피 연습)

• Strawberry and Chocolate Crepes

Utensils

1. 1 cup

2. 2 bowls

3. 1 frying pan

4. 1 wooden spoon

5. 1 spatula

6. 1 metal spoon

7. 1 plate

Ingredients

1. Two cups of flour
2. Three eggs
3. ¼ cup of butter
4. Three table spoons of sugar
5. Three cups of milk
6. One jar of Nutella chocolate spread
7. One box of fresh strawberries

 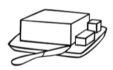

Directions

Put the numbers in cooking order.

Put the Nutella and strawberries on ½ of the pancake.

Mix the flour, eggs and sugar in a big bowl

Put the pancake batter into the frying-pan using a wooden spoon.

Put the pancake on a plate.

Fold the pancake over and then one more time to make a small △.

Serve your pancake and eat it!

Cook the pancakes for 1-3 minutes on low heat.

2. Kitchen Utensil (조리기구)

주방용 소도구는 요리에 필요한 주방 기물을 의미하며 주로 금속, 나무, 동, 철, 플라스틱, 유리 등으로 만들어진다. 가격이 상대적으로 저렴하고, 소모성이며 열원 (energy)을 필요로 하지 않는다.

1) 주방 조리용

① Cooking Ware(= Kitchen Ware로 Kitchen Appliances) : 순수한 조리 용으로 주방에서 요리를 할 때 사용하는 도구이다. 칼, 도마, 냄비, 프라이 팬, 볼 등 종류는 수십 가지이며 직접 조리에 이용되는 소모성 비품이다.

② Bakeware : 빵을 구울 때 사용되는 도구로 주로 오븐(Oven) 안에서 사용 한다.

2) 서비스용 (Service Ware)

조리 이후 음식이나 음료가 담겨 고객에게 직접 제공되는 도구이다. 식기를 비 롯하여 젓가락, 숟가락, 포크, 나이프, 커피 컵, 맥주잔, 술잔 등 테이블에 세팅 되어 고객이 직접 사용하는 수백 가지의 기물이 있다. 이러한 종류 이외에 서비스 서비스용 트레이(Service Tray), 음식집게(Tongue) 및 뷔페 준비물이 다수 있다. 큰 의미로 Tableware라고 하며 테이블에 직접 올려지는 기물로 접시류를 포함하여 유리(Glassware), 은기물류(Silverware), 도기류(Porcelain), 철기물류(Cutlery) 등이 있다.

① Dishware : 서빙 때나 음식을 먹을 때 사용되는 것으로 접시(Plate)나 볼(Bowl) 등이 있다.

② Drink-ware/Beverage-ware : 음료(Beverage)나 술(Liquor) 등을 담을 때 사용하는 기물이다.

③ Flate : 포크와 나이프류 같이 납작한 종류의 기물을 말한다.

④ Earthenware : 도자기류를 말한다. Pottery tableware와 같은 의미이다.

⑤ Silverware : 은박 도금을 표면에 입힌 것으로 철기물류(Cutlery), 편평한 기물류(Flatware) 등이 있다.

3) Knife

가장 기본적인 주방 소도구로 용도에 따라 아주 다양하게 사용된다. 서양식, 동양식의 칼이 각기 다르며 용도별로도 아주 세분화되어 있다. 서양식 칼의 경우 일반 요리용, 고기 절단용, 생선용, 토막내기용, 치즈용, 과일속파기용, 카빙용 등으로 세분화되며 동양식의 경우, 일식, 한식, 중국식 칼이 있으며 그 모양과 용도가 각기 다르다.

① 셰프나이프(Chef's Knife) : '조리사용 칼'이라 함. 프렌치 나이프라고도 한다. 요리 시 가장 광범위하게 다목적으로 사용되는 칼로서 고기나 야채 및 과일 등을 자르고 써는 용도로 이용된다.

② 중화요리용 칼(Chinese kitchen knife) : 중국, 베트남 등 주변 아시아 국가들에서 쓰이는 다목적 용 칼이다.

③ 뼈 발라내는 칼(**Boning knife**) : 날카로운 끝과 좁은 칼날로서 모든 종류의 육류와 생선류의 뼈를 제거하는 사용된다.

④ 빵 자르기용 칼(**Bread Knife**) : 빵 자르는 데 사용되는 칼

⑤ 기타(**Others**) : 과도(Paring knife), 버터용 칼(Butter knife), 고기전용 칼(Meat knife), 카빙용 칼(Carving knife), 슬라이서(Slicer), 일본요리의 회칼(Japanese Sashimi Knife), 일본 채소용 칼(Deba Knife), 한국의 막칼 등 다양하다.

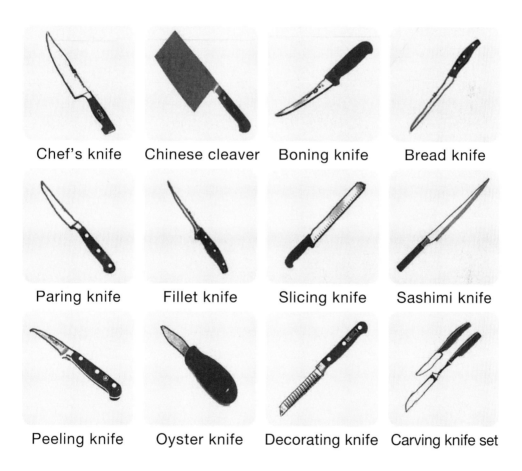

Chef's knife   Chinese cleaver   Boning knife   Bread knife

Paring knife   Fillet knife   Slicing knife   Sashimi knife

Peeling knife   Oyster knife   Decorating knife   Carving knife set

4) Pots & Pans

불을 사용할 때 가장 많이 사용하는 것이 Frypan이다. 주철팬(Cast iron pan)에서 시작하여 알루미늄팬(AL.), 스테인리스 스틸 팬(S/S), 구리팬(Copper), 전기식 프라이팬, 금속제 냄비(Braziere), 중탕기(Bain martie pot) 등 다양하게 발전되었다.

| Fry pan | Sauce pan | Chinese wok | Oblong fish kettle |

| Stock pot | Sauce pot | Pie pan | Round Pan |

| Griddle | Roasting pan | Bain martie pot | Sheet pan |

5) Tools for Food Preparation (기타, 음식 준비에 필요한 도구들)

주방용 조리기구는 매우 많다. 도구가 있으면 편리한 현실을 감안할 때 최적의 도구를 갖추는 일은 매우 중요하다. 각 도구의 영문 이름과 이용법을 숙지하여 가장 효율적인 주방 업무가 이루어지도록 하여야 할 것이다.

Peeler

Whisk

Ladle

Mixing bowl

Scoop

Measuing spoon

Lemon squeezer

Tong

Sieve

Scissor

Dough scraper

Spatula

Colander(Strainer)

Grater

(Ice cream) Disher

Slotted spoon

Melon baller

Dough cutter

Egg slicer

CHECK for Kitchen Utensils

1. 다음 그림의 명칭을 영어로 적으시오.

2. Boning Knife에 대하여 설명하라.

3. Cooking ware와 Service Ware의 차이점에 대하여 설명하라.

4. Lemon Squeezer의 용도는 무엇인가?

More on Utensils

Gadgets, Utensils and Other Equipment

Vegetable Peeler   Microplane Grater   Box Grater   Garlic Press   Juicer   Timer   Potato Masher

Pastry Scraper   Instant Read Thermometer   Mixing Bowls   Prep Bowls   Fine Stainer   Colander

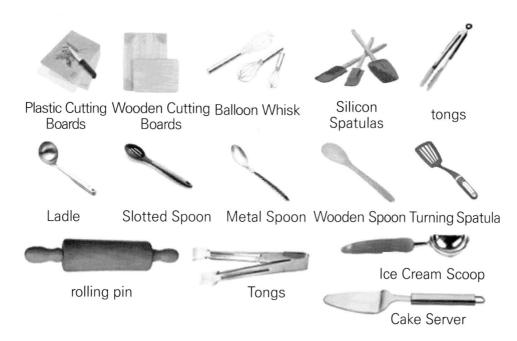

Plastic Cutting Boards　Wooden Cutting Boards　Balloon Whisk　Silicon Spatulas　tongs

Ladle　Slotted Spoon　Metal Spoon　Wooden Spoon　Turning Spatula

rolling pin　Tongs　Ice Cream Scoop　Cake Server

출처 https://www.easypacelearning.com/all-lessons/learning-english-level-1/1100-kitchen-utensils-equipment-learning-english

3. About Beef

소는 농가에 노동력을 제공해 주는 것 외에도 하나부터 열까지 자신의 모든 것을 사람들에게 주고 가는 아주 소중한 자원이자 먹을 거리이다.

1) Beef Cuts

쇠고기는 아주 다양한 부위로 나누어진 다음 요리에 이용된다. 요리가 발달한 프랑스는 35부위, 일본 및 중국은 15부위, 동아프리카는 51부위인 반면에 우리나라는 120여 부위로 구분해 사용하고 있다.

2) 나라별 구분

(1) 한국식 도체 구분의 예

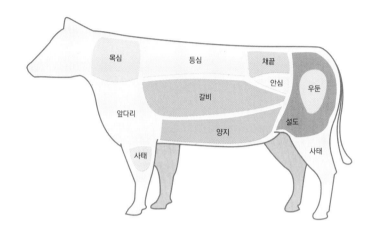

❶ 등심, 꽃등심, 살치살 : 등골뼈에 붙은 살코기로서 갈비뼈의 바깥쪽에 위치하는 부위로서, 구이, 스테이크, 전골용

❷ 목심 : 고깃결이 거친 편이나 맛 성분이 많다. 불고기, 탕

❸ 앞다리살, 갈비 덧살, 부채살(낙엽살) : 운동량이 많아 질기다. 육회, 스튜, 장조림

❹ 갈비, 갈빗살, 마구리, 토시살, 안창살, 제비추리 : 갈비, 찜, 탕, 구이용

❺ 양지, 업진살, 차돌백이, 치마살 : 가슴에서 배 아래쪽까지 이르는 부위로 지방이 많다. 구이, 탕

❻ 사태, 아롱사태 : 다리의 오금에 붙은 부위. 육회, 탕, 찜, 장조림용

❼ 우둔, 우둔살, 홍두깨살 : 엉덩이 부위. 산적, 장조림, 육포, 불고기

❽ 설도, 보섭살, 설깃살, 도가니살 : 뒷다리쪽 부위. 산적, 장조림, 육포용

❾ 채끝 : 허리뼈(등심 부분의 방아살 아래)를 감싸고 있는 부위로 육질이 부드럽고 지방이 많다. 스테이크용

❿ 안심 : 육질이 가장 연한 최상품. 고급 스테이크, 구이

(2) 미국식 도체 구분의 예

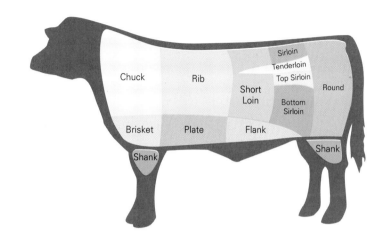

① 등심 Sirloin　　　② 목심 Chuck　　　③ 앞다리 Shank

④ 갈비 Rib　　　　　⑤ 양지 Brisket　　　⑥ 티본 T-Bone

⑦ 우둔 Round　　　　⑧ 설도 Shank　　　　⑨ 채끝 Striploin

⑩ 안심 Tenderloin

3) 굽기 정도의 표현

스테이크를 구울 때는 고객의 주문에 의하여 익힘 정도를 조절해야 한다. 이것은 사람마다 식성이 다르기 때문이다. 한국인들은 Welldone을 선호하는 편이지만, 일반적으로 외국인들은 Medium과 Medium Welldone을 가장 선호한다. Medium의 경우 고기 온도는 63~68℃ 정도이며 단면을 잘랐을 때 중앙이 핑크색이며 표면으로 갈수록 색이 갈색이 된다. 다음은 익힌 정도에 따른 분류이다.

1. **Very rare**　115~125℉ (46~52℃) Blood-red meat, soft, slightly juicy

2. **Rare**　125~135℉ (52~57℃) Red center, gray surface, soft, juicy

3. **Medium rare**   135~145℉ (57~63℃) Dark Pink throughout, gray-brown surface, very juicy

4. **Medium**   135~145℉ (63~68℃) Pink center, becomes gray-brown towards surface

5. **Medium well**   155~165℉ (68~74℃) Thin line of pink, firm texture

6. **Well done**   165℉ (74℃) Gray-brown throughout, tough texture, dry

식당에서는 고기를 주문한 고객과 아래와 같은 대화가 이루어진다.

Waiter(Waitress)	How would you like your steak, sir(or madam)?
Customer	Medium, please.

4) 마블링 고기 (Marbled meat)

마블링(Marbling)은 고기의 무늬가 대리석 무늬(marble pattern)를 닮았다고 해서 붙여진 이름으로서, 적색 고기 내에 퍼져 있는 지방을 말한다. 지방 교잡이 좋은 고기는 적당히 성숙하고 비육이 잘된 것으로 연하고 맛도 역시 좋다. 고기의 지방은 고기의 풍미와 식욕을 돋구는데 중요한 역할을 하는 것으로서 백색, 유백색, 크림색, 황색 등 여러 가지가 있다. 그 중 유백색의 광택을 띠면서 적당한 부드러움과 탄력을 지닌 것이 가장 좋다.

4. Cuisine Quiz (조리 퀴즈)

1. Roasting is a basic cooking method. A very important principle of roasting is that you cook with   .

　a. Dry heat 　　　　b. Steam heat 　　　c. Direct flame

2. When roasting, you should not add water or cover the roast. How can you keep the roast from stewing in its own juices?

　a. There are no juices to worry about.

　b. Drain off the juices from time to time.

　c. Place the roast on a rack.

3. It is very important to know when a roast is done. Which is the most reliable way?

　a. Cook for the time shown on a meat chart.

　b. Feel the firmness of the roast.

　c. Use a thermometer.

UNIT 13 Broiling

Part 1 · English Skill Up

1. Vocabulary Preview
2. Reading
3. Review Exercises
4. English for Fun

Part 2 · Culinary English

1. Recipe Reading & Writing Exercise(레시피 연습)
2. English for Fun
3. Cuisine Quiz(조리 퀴즈)

Part 1 — **English Skill Up**

1. Vocabulary Preview 🎧

dip	적시다	stick	달라붙다
sear	강열에 쪼이다	juice	육즙
seal	봉하다	intense	강렬한
shrink	수축하다	tasteless	맛없는
flame	불꽃	char	태우다
spoil	망치다	appearance	외양
	집게	stab	찌르다
		fatty	기름기 있는
tongs		juiciness	육즙 보존
		squeeze	짜다, 압착하다
puncture	구멍을 내다		

2. Reading 🎧

BROILING

The rules and procedures for correct broiling.

1) Dip the steak in cooking oil. The oil prevents sticking and aids in browning.

2) Sear the steak

① The steaks are seared on the hot part of the grill, but they are not cooked there.

② The juices are sealed into the meat by the intense heat.

③ The intense heat will cause shrinking, and drying and the steak will be dry and tasteless.

④ So you should move them to the cooler part of the grill to finish cooking.

⑤ Flames add some flavor to meats, but too much flame will char your meats, spoiling both their appearance and taste.

3) For X-markings on the meat

Turn the steak to a different angle - this causes the X-markings on the meat, adding to the eye appeal.

Learn the art of marking broiled meats. It takes practice, but it pays off.

4) Use tongs instead of a fork.

Every time you stab a steak with a fork, the juices will run out.

If you must use a fork, use it in the fatty edge of the meat

5) Juiciness is the secret of its flavor.

Protect the juiciness of steaks. Don't puncture steaks or squeeze them.

In handling the steak, never press down on it; the only time you should press down on the steak is when it is tested to see if it is done.

6) Coordination with the serving staff

- It is not a good practice to hold steaks at the side of the broiler when they are done, for the continuing heat can only dry them out.
- If your coordination is working well, the waiter/waitress should be ready to pick them up the moment they are finished.

• Reading Helper

Broiling. (직화 석쇠구이 조리법)

1) 스테이크를 식용 오일에 적신다. 오일은 고기가 석쇠에 달라붙지 못하게 하고 갈색으로 변하게 촉진시킨다.

2) 스테이크를 강열에 잠시 쪼인다. (Searing)

① 스테이크는 석쇠의 강열 부분에서 잠시 searing 하지만 거기에서 익히지는 않는다.

- Searing : 고기 표면에 잠시 강열을 쪼여 기공(pore)을 막아 육즙을 보호하고 연한 갈색으로 변하게 하는 조리법

② 강열에 쫓겨 육즙이 고기 속으로 들어가고 봉해진다.

③ 강열은 스테이크를 위축, 메마르고, 무미건조하게 만든다.

④ 스테이크를 온도가 낮은 쪽으로 옮겨 그곳에서 익힌다.

⑤ 불꽃은 향을 돋구지만 지나치면 고기 표면을 태워 보기 싫고 맛도 없어진다.

3) X-markings (격자무늬 만들기)

- 스테이크를 다른 각도로 돌려놓으면 고기 표면에 격자 무늬가 생겨 시각적인 매력을 더한다.
- 오랜 수련이 필요하지만 그만한 보람이 따른다.

4) 포크 대신 집게 사용. 스테이크가 찔려 육즙이 흘러나오므로.

- 포크 사용할 경우엔 기름 많은 쪽에서 사용

5) 육즙 보존이 향취의 비결

- 육즙 보존을 위해 스테이크를 찌르거나 짓누르지 말 것
- 스테이크가 다 익었는지 테스트할 때 단 한 번 누를 것

6) 서빙 스탭과 긴밀한 협조

- 다 익었는데 broiler 위에 그대로 두면 계속 열을 받아 건조해진다.
- 고기가 익으면 즉시 서빙하도록 한다.

3. Review Exercises

1) Put the following into Korean.

dip		stick	
sear		juice	
seal		intense	
shrink		tasteless	
flame		char	
spoil		appearance	
tongs		stab	

fatty		juiciness	
squeeze		puncture	

2) Put the following into Korean.

1. Dip the steak in cooking oil. The oil prevents sticking and aids in browning.

2. Sear the steak The steaks are seared on the hot part of the grill, but they are not cooked there.

3. The juices are sealed into the meat by the intense heat.

4. The intense heat will cause shrinking, and drying and the steak will be dry and tasteless.

5. Learn the art of marking broiled meats. It takes practice, but it pays off.

6. Use tongs instead of a fork. Every time you stab a steak with a fork, the juices will run out.

4. English for Fun

• Cooking Vocabulary Definitions (조리기구 퀴즈)

Choose the correct definition for the cooking vocabulary in this quiz.

1. What is the definition of <u>Cupboard</u>?

   a. The different parts of a meal.
   b. An activity that has taken place over a long period of time and is always done the same way.
   c. A holder for dishes after they have been washed (similar to dish rack).
   d. An enclosed space that is used for storage.

2. What is the definition of <u>Flavor</u>?

   a. A type of energy that can be used to produce heat and light.
   b. The taste of something.
   c. A type of fuel used for cooking with an open flame.
   d. The top of a cooker for cooking food contained in pans (similar to a stove).

3. What is the definition of <u>Mixer</u>?

   a. To select the correct amount of something.

b. A machine to stir ingredients (same as food processor).

c. To be half or partially cooked.

d. A type of pan that seals and can cook at very high temperatures.

4. What is the definition of Sieve?

a. An object with small holes in it for separating objects.

b. To be pleasing or relevant.

c. To have a hot flavor.

d. Two pieces of bread with a filling between them.

Part 2 — Culinary English

1. Recipe Reading & Writing Exercise (레시피 연습)

1) Chocolate Chip Cookies

Read the recipe below, and then answer the questions that follow.

Ingredients

½ cup	margarine or butter flavored Crisco
½ cup	brown sugar
½ cup	white sugar
1 ea	egg
½ tsp	vanilla extract
1 cup	plus 2 tbs flour
½ tsp	salt
½ tsp	baking soda
1 pkg	mini chocolate chips

Directions

1. Mix margarine or Crisco, sugar and brown sugar.

2. Mix in egg and vanilla.

3. Mix in baking soda, salt and then flour.

4. Dump in the chocolate chips.

5. Mix. Bake at 350F for 10-12 minutes.

Questions

1. What kind of cookies is this recipe for?

2. What is the third step in this recipe?

3. If you doubled this recipe, how much vanilla extract and flour would you need?

4. How long should the cookies be baked? At what temperature?

5. List other ingredients you could add to this recipe to make it more scrumptious.

2) 요리 단계에 따른 기본 표현

(1) 준비 단계

- 파슬리를 곱게 다져라. **Chop the parsley finely.**
- 양파를 가늘게 썰어라. **Slice the onions thinly.**
- 셀러리 껍질을 벗기고 슬라이스하라. **Peel and slice the celery.**
- 고기를 작은 주사위 모양으로 자르라. **Cut meats into small dice.**
- 반으로 자르라. **Cut into halves.**
- 마늘 한 쪽을 으깨라. **Crush a clove of garlic.**
- 볼에서 모든 재료를 고루 잘 섞어라. **Mix in all the ingredients in bowl.**
- 레몬을 뒤틀어서 즙을 짜라. **Twist to squeeze the lemon out.**

(2) 요리 단계

- 고기가 부드러워질 때까지 천천히 요리하라. **Simmer the meat until tender.**
- 부드럽고 투명해질 때까지 요리하라. **Cook until tender and transparent.**
- 계란이 거품이 일어날 때까지 쳐올려라. **Beat the eggs until frothy.**

(3) 가열 단계

- 팬에서 버터를 녹여라. **Melt the butter in pan.**
- 팬에서 기름을 달구어라. **Heat the oil in pan.**
- 양파와 당근을 팬에 넣어라. **Put the onion and carrot into the pan.**
- 당근, 감자, 셀러리 및 양파의 순으로 볶아라. **Saute carrot, potato, celery and onion in turn.**
- 반죽을 치대어 부드럽게 만들어라. **Knead dough until smooth.**

(4) 마감 단계

- 간을 하라. **Adjust seasoning.**
- 소금, 후추로 간을 하라. **Season with salt and pepper to taste.**
- 파슬리로 장식하라. **Garnish with parsley**
- 파슬리 다진 것을 뿌려라. **Sprinkle with chopped parsley.**
- 수프를 볼로 옮겨라. **Transfer the soup to a soup bowl.**

(5) 보관 및 저장 단계

- 상온에서 보관하라. **Keep in the room temperature.**
- 식힌 다음 냉장하라. **Make it cool and refrigerate.**
- 냉장고에서 보관하라. **Keep in the refrigerator.**
- 냉동시켜라. **Keep in the freezer.**
- 식초와 오일을 항아리 속에 넣어라. **Place the vinegar and oil in a jar.**

2. English for Fun

• Grammar Tips : 'Is' and 'Are'

Fill in the blanks from the given phrases.

> where's, it is (2), here are, here's, they are, where are

Husband	Where are the tomatoes?
Wife	Here _____ .
Husband	And where's the cheese?
Wife	Here _____ .
Husband	And how about the eggs?
	_____ the eggs?
Wife	Here they are. Don't drop them!
Husband	Don't worry.
Wife	Do you need anything else?
Husband	Yes. _____ the milk?
Wife	It's right here.
Husband	Hmm. Let me see. Oh, yes. Is there any celery?
Wife	Yes. Here _____ . What are you making?
Husband	Count/Non-Count Nouns.
Wife	What?!
Husband	Count/Non-Count Nouns! It's a recipe in this new

cookbook. Here. Take a look.

Wife   It looks delicious.

Husband It's healthy, too. It's full of nutritious nouns.

Wife   What else do you need?

Husband I think I have everything else.   the
         onions. Here are the beans, Here's the salt, and
                  the pepper.

Wife   I can't wait to taste it!

3. Cuisine Quiz (조리 퀴즈)

1. The broiler chef's tools should include a pair of tongs and a
   broiling fork. Which is the preferred tool for handling steak?

   a. Tongs   b. Fork

2. You should not press down on steaks when handling them.
   Press them with a fork or your finger for the following purpose
   only   .

   a. To taste them   b. To test for doneness
   c. Never press them

3. If you hold steak at the side of the broiler when it is done, the
   steak will   .

   a. Cool down   b. Overcook   c. Dry out

CHAPTER 4

Story of Food

Unit·14 Potatoes
Unit·15 Chocolate
Unit·16 Mustard

학습목표

동서양을 막론하고 대표적인 식품인 감자(potatoes), 초콜릿(chocolate), 그리고 겨자(mustard)의 유래에 관한 글을 읽고 내용을 파악하고, 단계별로 학습한 내용을 바탕으로 레시피를 본격적으로 작성할 수 있다.

UNIT 14 Potatoes

Part 1 · English Skill Up

1. Vocabulary Preview
2. Reading
3. Review Exercises
4. English for Fun

Part 2 · Culinary English

1. Recipe Reading & Writing Exercise(레시피 연습)
2. Expression of Tastes
3. My Favorite Recipe(내가 좋아하는 레시피)
4. Cuisine Quiz(조리 퀴즈)

Part 1 — English Skill Up

1. Vocabulary Preview 🎧

imagine	상상하다	instead	대신에
poison	독	disease	질병
dish	요리	baked	구운
invent	발명하다	ketchup	케첩

2. Reading 🎧

Potatoes

Can you imagine life without French fries? Potatoes are very popular today. But in the past this was not true. Potatoes grew in South America five thousand years ago. But they only became popular in other places two hundred years ago.

In the 16th century, the Spanish took the potato from South America to Europe. But the people in Europe did not like this strange vegetable. Some people thought that if you ate the potato your skin would look like the skin of a potato. Other people could not believe that you ate the underground part of the plant. So they ate the leaves instead. This make them sick because there is poison in the leaves.

In the 1800s people started to eat potatoes. In Ireland potatoes became the main food. Then, in 1845, a disease killed all the potatoes in Ireland. Two million people died of hunger.

Today, each country has its potato dish. Germans eat potato salad, and the United States has the baked potato. And, of course, the French invented French fries. Now French fries are popular all over the world. The English eat them with salt and vinegar, the French eat them with salt and pepper, and the Americans with ketchup.

• Looking for the Main Ideas

Choose the best answer.

1. Potatoes are   .

   a. popular today

   b. not popular today

   c. never popular

2. In the 16th century, people in Europe

                          .

   a. like the potato

   b. had bad skin

   c. did not like the potato

3. People started to   .

   a. eat potatoes in the 1800s

   b. kill potatoes in the 1800s

   c. go the Ireland in the 1800s

4. French fries are   .

   a. salt and pepper

   b. popular all over the world

   c. from Germany

3. Review Exercises

1) Put the following into English

imagine	instead
poison	disease
dish	baked
invent	ketchup

2) Complete the sentences with the correct word.

1. When you have a picture in your mind about something, you   .

   a. imagine   b. grow

2. When you want something in place of something else, you want it   .

   a. soon   b. instead

3. A person can get sick or die if he/she takes or eats   .

   a. poison   b. salt

4. A sickness that passes from one person to another is a   .

   a. disease   b. hunger

5. Special cooked food of one kind is called a   .

   a. salad   b. dish

6. A whole potato with its skin, cooked in an oven is   .

   a. fried   b. baked

7. When you think of or make something for the first time, you

   .

   a. become   b. invent

8. The tomato sauce that you usually buy in a bottle is called

   .

   a. vinegar   b. ketchup

3) Looking for the details

One word in each sentence is not correct. Rewrite the sentence with the correct word.

1. Potatoes grew in Europe five thousand years ago.

2. In the 18th century, the Spanish took the potato to Europe.

3. There is poison in the skin of the potato.

4. A disease killed the people in Ireland in 1845.

5. Five million people died of hunger in Ireland.

6. Germany has the baked potato.

7. The Americans invented French fries.

4. English for Fun

• Grammar Tips: Measuring Words

Work in Pairs.

1. What kind of food do you buy at the supermarket?

2. How many cups of coffee do you drink every day?

3. What kind of dessert do you like?

4. How much milk do you drink every day?

Put the following into English.

1. 빵 한 덩어리를 저에게 사 주시겠습니까?

2. 사과 1 파운드에 얼마입니까?

3. 저는 사과 파이 한 조각과 커피 한 잔을 마셨습니다.

4. 프라이팬(pan)에 약간의 버터와 몇 개의 양파를 넣으세요.

Part 2 — Culinary English

1. Recipe Reading & Writing Exercise(레시피 연습)

• Recipe Writing Exercise

The following is a recipe for a hamburger. Number the sentences in the correct order.

Then, add some ketchup

Later, put the meat on the bread

Afterward, put an onion ring on top of the cheese

Preparing a burger

First, slice tomato and onion

After that, place the cheese on top of the meat

Next, spread mayonaise on the bread

Then, add lettuce and tomato

Finally, cover with a second loaf of bread and enjoy

Now write your own recipe. You need to include words such as first, then, later and next.

1.

2.

3.

4.

5.

6.

7.

8.

9.

2. Expressions for Tastes

맛을 나타내는 표현들

음식의 맛은 Taste(혀로 보는 맛), Flavor(코로 맡는 냄새나 방향), Savor(일반적인 풍미) 등이 있다.

1) 기본적인 맛 (혀의 감각)

(1) 달콤한 : Sweet, sugary

- 단맛이 나는 간장 : Sweet and mild soy sauce
- 단맛이 나는 와인 : Sweet wine
- 달콤새콤한 : Sweet and sour
- 달콤매콤한 : Sweetly tangy
- 달콤한 냄새가 나다 : Smell sweet, be fragrant

이 초콜릿은 달콤한 냄새가 난다 : This chocolate smells sweet.

(2) 짠 : Salty, salted, a salty taste

- 짠맛 나는 간장 : Salty soy sauce

(3) 쓴 : Bitter

- 쓴 약 : a bitter medicine
- 맥주의 씁쓸한 맛 : the slight bitterness of beer
- 약간 쓴맛이 나다 : be (taste) slightly bitter
- 달콤씁쓸한 : Bitter-sweet
- 블랙 커피는 내게 너무 쓰다 : Black coffee is too bitter for me.

(4) 새콤한, 신맛이 나는 : Sour, acid, tart

- 신 포도 : a sour grape
- 신 레몬 : an acid lemon
- 신 사과 : a tart apple
- 이 사과는 시큼한 냄새가 난다 : This apple have sour taste.

(5) 매운, 자극성이 있는, 얼얼한 : Hot, spicy, pungent, spicy, tangy, pepperish

- 매운 김치 : hot kimchi
- 톡 쏘는 매콤한 소스 : a rich and pungent sauce
- 이 카레는 내겐 너무 맵다 : This curry is too hot for me.

(6) 떫은 : astringent, harsh

- 떫은 감 : an astringent persimmon
- 떫은 와인 : rough(harsh) wine

2) 감정의 맛 (느낌 및 표현의 맛)

❶ 군침이 도는 : Mouth watering

❷ 아삭한(바삭바삭한) : Crispy, Crunchy

❸ (좋은) 향이 나는 : Aromatic

❹ 과일 향이 나는 : Fruity

❺ 훈제(훈연)냄새가 나는 : Smokey

❻ 부드러운, 연한 : Soft, smooth, mild, mellow → (반대말) Chewy(질긴), Hard(딱딱한, 견고한)

❼ 매끄러운 : Smooth → (반대말) Hard, Coarse(딱딱한, 거친)

❽ (고기 등이) 연한 : Tender → (반대말) Tough (질긴, 굳은, 단단한)

❾ (크림같이) 매끈하고 부드러운 : Creamy → (반대말) Crumbly(부서지기 쉬운, 푸석푸석한)

❿ 탄력이 있는 : Springy, Elastic

⓫ 즙이 많은, 수분이 있는, 촉촉한 : Juicy, Moist, Soggy → (반대말) Dry(마른, 건조한)

⓬ 묽은, 얇은(가는) : Thin → (반대말) Thick

⓭ 진한, 굵은 : Thick → (반대말) Thin 예) Thick Soup (진한 수프)

⓮ 날것의 (생 것의) : Raw → (반대말) Well done, Cooked(요리가 된, 잘 익은)

⓯ 끈적끈적한 : Sticky → (반대말) Hard(딱딱한)

⓰ (표면이) 투명한, 광택이 나는 : Transparent → (반대말) Opaque(광택이 없는, 칙칙한)

⓱ 싱싱한, 산뜻한 : Fresh

⓲ 최상급의, 특등품의 : Top, Best, Excellent, Super, Supreme

⓳ 맛있는 : Delicious, Tasty → (반대말) Tasteless(맛이 없는)

⑳ 풍미가 있는 : Palatable, Savory

㉑ 특제의, 특별한 : Special

㉒ 맛깔스런 : Agreeable

㉓ 담백한 : Plain, Simple

㉔ 느끼한, 위에 부담스러운 : Heavy

㉕ (음식이) 초라한, 보잘것없는 : Poor

3) 맛에 대한 간단한 표현

(1) 맛이 있다(좋다)

- be tasty(savory)
- taste good(nice)
- have a good flavor
- be delicious

(2) 맛이 없다(나쁘다)

- be untasty
- taste bad
- flat
- be unsavory
- be unpalatable
- be flavorless (insipid, jejune)

(3) ~으로 간을 하다

season food with salt and pepper.

(4) ~의 맛이 나다

taste [savor] of orange.

(5) 맛이 변하다

become stale.

(6) 맛이 시게 변하다

turn sour

(7) 맛이 어떻습니까?

How does it taste? or What does it taste like?

(8) 먹어 봐야 맛을 안다

The proof of the pudding is in eating.

4) 표현 예문

❶ 군침 돌게 하는 석쇠구이한 닭가슴살 : Mouth watering charcoal grilled chicken breast

❷ (농도가 연한) 콩소메 : Thin consomme

❸ 아삭아삭한 양상추 : Crispy lettuce

❹ 부드러운 치즈 : Soft cheese

❺ 입에서 녹는 달콤한 티라미수(이태리 치즈케이크) : Sweet tiramisu

❻ 크림같이 (줄줄 흐르는) 소스를 곁들인 푸딩 : Creamy pudding

❼ 오븐에서 갓 구운 신선한 빵 : freshly baked bread

❽ 특등품의 한우 안심 : Supreme Korean beef tenderloin

❾ 얼얼한 맛이 나는 김치 전골 : Spicy Kimchi Casserole

⑩ (농도가 진한) 곰탕 : Thick Gomtang

⑪ (엄선한) 최상급의 오리 가슴살 : Selected special Duck breast

⑫ 맛깔스런 탕수육 : An agreeable Sweet and sour beef

⑬ 갓 잡아 올린 싱싱한 모듬 해물회 : Assorted raw fish sashimi

⑭ 감칠맛이 나는 복어 맑은 탕 : Savory taste of Japanese global fish soup

3. My Favorite Recipe (내가 좋아하는 레시피)

• Chocolate chip cookie (make 18 cookies)

Ingredients

120g	unsalted butter
55g	white sugar
115g	dark brown sugar
½tsp	salt
1ea	egg
1tsp	vanilla extract
200g	AP flour
½tsp	baking soda
150g	chocolate chip

Directions

1. Scale all ingredients with a digital scale. Sift flour and baking soda together. Preheat the oven to 170℃.

2. In a bowl, softened butter, white and dark brown sugar and salt. Creaming together for 10 minutes.

3. Add an egg and vanilla extract. Mix them well with a beater until smooth.

4. Add dry ingredients and combine them thoroughly with a spatula.

5. Pour chocolate chips into a batter and combine.

6. Scoop out the dough with an ice cream scoop onto a sheet pan lined with parchment paper. Baker them at 170℃ for 10 to 12 minutes.

Notes		
unsalted 소금기를 뺀	extract 추출액
flour 밀가루 AP flour	scale 저울에 달다
sift 체로 걸러내다	preheat 예열하다
thoroughly 철저히	spatula 주걱, 프라이뒤집개
batter 반죽	scoop 국자로 떠내다
parchment paper 기름종이	

4. Cuisine Quiz(조리 퀴즈)

1. You should carry hot containers with which kind of towels?

a. Wet   b. Dry

2. You should be careful when lighting a gas oven. It is possible for unburned gas to accumulate in the oven. Before turning on the gas,

a. Leave the door open for a moment.
b. Check for the smell of gas.
c. Don't open the door.

UNIT 15 Chocolates

Part 1 · English Skill Up

1. Vocabulary Preview
2. Reading
3. Review Exercises
4. English for Fun

Part 2 · Culinary English

1. Recipe Reading & Writing Exercise(레시피 연습)
2. My Favorite Recipe(내가 좋아하는 레시피)
3. Cuisine Quiz(조리 퀴즈)

Part 1 — English Skill Up

1. Vocabulary Preview 🎧

hot chili peppers	매운 칠리고추
bitter	쓰라린, 쓴맛의
add	더하다
discover	발견하다
chemical	화학물질

2. Reading 🎧

Chocolate

The Aztecs of Mexico knew about chocolate a long time ago. They made it into a drink. Sometimes they put hot chili peppers with the chocolate. They called the drink "xocoatl" which means "bitter juice." This is where the word chocolate" comes from.

The Spanish took the drink from the land of the Aztecs to Europe. The Spanish didn't like peppers so they added sugar to the chocolate. This drink became very popular in Europe. Until 1850 chocolate was only a drink. After that time Europeans discovered that chocolate was good to eat too.

The Aztecs believed that chocolate make you intelligent. Today, we do not believe this. But chocolate has a special chemical - phenylethylamine. This is the same chemical the

phenylethylamine. This is the same chemical the body make when a person is in love. Which do you prefer? Chocolate or being in love?

• Looking for the Main Ideas

Choose the best answer.

1. The Aztecs made   .

   a. chili peppers into a drink

   b. chocolate into a drink

   c. chocolate peppers

2. The Spanish   .

   a. discovered chocolate

   b. gave chocolate to the Aztecs

   c. took the chocolate drink to Europe

3. Chocolate   .

   a. has a special chemical

   b. has no special chemicals

   c. makes you love chemicals

3. Review Exercises

1) Put the following into English.

hot chili peppers	bitter
add	discover
chemical	

2) Complete the sentences with the correct word.

1. When peppers burn your mouth like fire, they are _____ .

   a. hot   b. bitter

2. The kinds of peppers that are hot and burn your mouth are called _____ .

   a. chocolate peppers   b. chili peppers

3. Something that has a taste like strong coffee without sugar is _____ .

   a. bitter   b. popular

4. When you put something with something else, you _____ it.

   a. like   b. add

5. When you find something that nobody knows before, you _____ it.

   a. believe   b. discover

6. Phenylethylamine is a _____ .

   a. chemical   b. drink

3) Looking for Details

Circle T if the sentence is true. Circle F if the sentence is false.

1. The Aztecs put sugar into the chocolate.   (T)   (F)

2. The word "chocolate" means bitter juice.   (T)   (F)

3. The Spanish took peppers to Europe.   (T)   (F)

4. In 1850, people began to eat chocolate.   (T)   (F)

5. Chocolate makes you intelligent.   (T)   (F)

6. Phenylethylamine is the chemical in chocolate.   (T)   (F)

4. English for Fun

• Grammar Tips: Much & Many

Work in Pairs.

1. Is there any bread in your house?

2. Are there any oranges in your house?

3. What's your favorite food?

4. What kinds of food are bad for your health?]

Put the following into English.

1. 우유가 없어요.

2. 계란이 없습니다.

3. 나는 쿠키를 너무 많이 먹는다.

4. 그녀는 커피를 너무 많이 마십니다.

Part 2 — **Culinary English**

1. Recipe Reading & Writing Exercise (레시피 연습)

• Recipe Writing Exercise

Pumpkin Soup

Ingredients

2 kg   .

.

500 ml   .

1 vegetable cube.

30g   .

To serve: 2 bread rolls.

Instructions

First, dice the pumpkin and chop the onions. Then, put 30 grams of butter into a sauce pan and heat it on medium heat. Next, add the onions and fry them until they are ok. After that, add the pumpkin and mix them well. Then, add water until they are all covered. Next, put the vegetable stock cube to the sauce pan and let it boil. After that, simmer until the pumpkin goes soft. Once it simmers, take the mixture and blend it well. Finally, put it back and heat it. The pumpkin soup is ready. Serve it with bread rolls.

2. My Favorite Recipe (내가 좋아하는 레시피)

• Grandmom's Apple Pie

Ingredients

5~6 cooking apples – Rome Apples are a good choice

3/4 cup sugar

3 tablespoons cornstarch

2 tablespoons lemon juice (or 1 tablespoon vinegar)

3 tablespoons cinnamon

1/4 teaspoon nutmeg

3 tablespoons butter

dash of salt

2 pie crusts (top and bottom)

Directions

Peel and slice apples. Add lemon juice, and toss. Sprinkle some of the sugar and cinnamon in the bottom of crust. Add 1 tablespoon of cornstarch. Put half of the apple slices in the crust. Repeat layering of apples, sugar, cinnamon, nutmeg, and cornstarch. Apples will pile high in pie crust. Dot with butter. Top apples with second crust. Seal crust. Cut vents in top. Bake 50 to 60 minutes or until done. Yield: 8 servings.

Notes		
cornstarch 녹말풀		cinnamon 계피
nutmeg 너트메그, 육두구		toss (피자를) 훌떡 뒤집다
sprinkle 뿌리다		seal 봉하다
vent 배출구, 배기구		

3. Cuisine Quiz (조리 퀴즈)

1. If you find steam leaking from a pipe joint or a valve, you should
_____ .

a. Report it to your supervisor.

b. Try to locate the shut-off valve.

c. Ignore it.

2. Don't handle broken glass with your bare hands, if possible.
Pick it up with a pan and a broom. The smaller slivers can be
picked up with _____ .

a. A vacuum cleaner.

b. A wet paper towel.

c. Neither.

UNIT 16 Mustard

Part 1 · English Skill Up

1. Vocabulary Preview
2. Reading
3. Review Exercises
4. English for Fun

Part 2 · Culinary English

1. Recipe Reading & Writing Exercise(레시피 연습)
2. My Favorite Recipe(내가 좋아하는 레시피)
3. Cuisine Quiz(조리 퀴즈)

Part 1 — English Skill Up

1. Vocabulary Preview 🎧

ancient	고대의
chest	가슴
rheumatism	류마티스
sauce	소스
seeds	씨
grind	갈다
spices	양념, 향료

mustard plant

pepper plant

2. Reading 🎧

Mustard

Mustard is a food that is three thousand years old. The ancient Egyptians and Chinese used it. Today the French must have it with beef. Americans like it on their hot dogs and hamburgers and often put it in sandwiches.

But mustard is famous not only as a food. For thousands of years people used mustard as medicine. In the United States people put mustard on their chest for a chest cold or used mustard for rheumatism. This kind of medicine is not so popular today.

The mustard plant is a pretty plant with bright yellow flowers. It grows easily everywhere. So how do we make this **yellow sauce** from it? We take the **seeds** of the plant. Then we **grind** the seeds and mix them with salt, spices, and vinegar. These **spices** are very important. Without them mustard will not have its bright yellow color.

• Looking for the Main Ideas

Choose the best answer.

1. Mustard is   .

    a. a new food

    b. an ancient food

    c. only a French food

2. Mustard is   .

    a. also famous as medicine

    b. popular as medicine today

    c. not famous as a food

3. Mustard comes from   .

    a. vinegar

    b. the seeds of the mustard plant

    c. yellow salt

3. Review Exercises

1) Put the following into English.

ancient	chest
rheumatism	sauce
seeds	grind
spices	

2) Complete the definitions. Circle the correct answer.

1. When something is from a very long time ago, it is   .

   a. Chinese   b. ancient

2. The upper front part of your body, where you can find your heart and lungs, is the   .

   a. beef   b. chest

3. A kind of disease that gives pain to muscles and bones is   .

   a. chest cold   b. rheumatism

4. A thick liquid you put on food is a   .

   a. sauce   b. spice

5. The part of a plant that grows into a new plant is a   .

   a. flower   b. seed

6. When you make seeds into a powder, you   them.

   a. grind   b. mix

3) Looking for Details

Circle T if the sentence is true. Circle F if the sentence is false.

1. Mustard is thirty thousand years old.　　(T)　　(F)

2. The Egyptians used it on hamburgers.　　(T)　　(F)

3. Mustard can be medicine.　　(T)　　(F)

4. People use mustard for chest colds.　　(T)　　(F)

5. Mustard plants grow only in China.　　(T)　　(F)

6. Spices give mustard its bright color.　　(T)　　(F)

Discussion

Discuss these questions with your classmates.

1. What is the most popular spice in your country?

2. What is your favorite spice?

3. Which spices are good for you?

4. Which spices do you not like? Why?

garlic   soy sauce   curry

chilli
peppers   ginger   salt

4. English for Fun

• Class Game: Twenty Questions

"What is it?"

Choose a leader.

Leader   Think of a food you like. Don't say it!

Class   Ask the leader YES/NO questions.

Leader   Answer "Yes" or "No."

Class   Try to guess the food. Whoever guesses is the new leader.

Part 2 — **Culinary English**

1. Recipe Reading & Writing Exercise (레시피 연습)

1) 레시피 단계별 실전연습

How we make a French Omelette?

Match the words with the pictures:

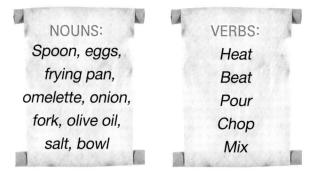

NOUNS:
Spoon, eggs, frying pan, omelette, onion, fork, olive oil, salt, bowl

VERBS:
Heat
Beat
Pour
Chop
Mix

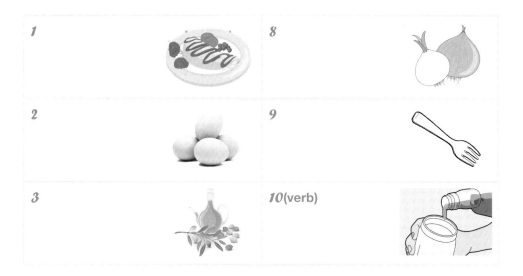

1		8	
2		9	
3		10(verb)	

4

5

6

7

11(verb)

12(verb)

13(verb)

14(verb)

2) Now look at the FRENCH OMELETTE RECIPE

Try to fill the gaps with the words in exercise 1:

Ingredients

2

1

5 spoons of olive

½ spoon of

How to Make an Egg Omelette:

First, the eggs in a bowl.

Add the chopped and .

 all of them in the .

Heat the olive oil in a and add the mixture

(the egg, the onion and the salt).

Cook with the help of a spoon and a in low heat, not very hot!

A TIP: Serve hot with a piece of .

2) Writing Your Own Recipe

• Tuna Sandwich

Ingredients

1 can of tuna

2 loaves of Bread

1 leaf of lettuce

Mayonnaise

1 slice of cheese

Now write a recipe. Choose the ingredients below:

2. My Favorite Recipe (내가 좋아하는 레시피)

• Sponge Cake (makes 1 cake)

Ingredients

60g butter, softened

1tsp vanilla **extract**

4 ea eggs

3 ea egg **yolks**

190g caster **sugar**

190g cake flour, **sifted**

Directions

1. Dust the cake pan with a bit of softened butter and some flour.

2. Combine the eggs and egg yolks, and sugar in a mixing bowl.

3. Set over a double boiler and whisk constantly until the caster sugar **dissolves**.

4. Whip the mixture in a stand mixer with a whisk attachment until the **foam** reaches maximum volume for 10 minutes.

5. **Reduce** the speed to low and mix for 15 minutes to **stabilize** the mixture.

6. Fold in the flour carefully. Fold in softened butter and vanilla extract.

7. Pour the cake **batter** into a round cake pan filling the pans two-thirds full.

8. Bake at 175℃ until the tops of the cakes spring back when touched, about 20-30 minutes.

9. Cool the cake in the pan for 5 minutes and then unmold onto a sheet pan.

10. Transfer the cake on a cooling rack and cool it completely.

Notes	
extract 추출액	yolk 노른자
caster sugar 정제설탕	sifted 체에 친
dissolve 녹다	foam 거품
reduce 줄이다	stabilize 안정화시키다
batter 반죽	unmold 틀에서 빼내다
transfer 전환하다	

3. Cuisine Quiz(조리 퀴즈)

1. If you can't lift a sack or carton comfortably, get help. If you have to move to a few steps, use   .

a. A sling or cradle.

b. A third helper.

c. A cart or a dolly.

2. For safety's sake, when you use a cart or dolly, be sure:

a. The boss knows you are using it.

b. You can see where you are going.

c. The cart is not overloaded.

부록

조리용어

부록: 조리용어

A

á Blacne 아 블랑 : '흰색으로' 란 의미로, 요리할 때 고기 색을 내지 않고 익히는 음식을 뜻한다.

Adobo 아도보 : 닭과 돼지고기를 볶아서 고추, 식초, 허브와 코코넛 우유를 넣어 만든 필리핀 음식을 말하며, 닭고기를 이용하여 만든 음식을 '치킨 아도보'라고 한다.

Aging 에이징 : 고기의 맛과 풍미를 증진시키기 위해 적절한 환경에서 숙성시키는 과정으로, 습기가 적은 34~38℉ 온도에서 3~6주 동안 저장하여 육질을 부드럽게 숙성시킨다.

Aioli 아이올리 : 남프랑스 프로방스 지방의 강한 마늘향의 마요네즈이다. 생선, 육류, 채소 등과 함께 이용한다.

a la 알라 : '~풍의, ~식으로'란 의미로 예를 들면, 알 라 부르귀뇽(a la bourguignonne)은 버건디(Burgundy)식으로 요리하라는 뜻이다.

a l'Ancienne 아 란시안 : '옛 방식의'란 의미의 프랑스어로, 쇠고기를 브레이징(braising)한 후 시머링(simmering)하는 방법 등을 말한다.

a l'Anglaise 아 랑글레즈 : 간단하게 데치거나 삶는 방식의 '영국식'을 의미하며, 빵가루를 입혀서 튀길 수도 있다.

á la Bourguignonne 알 라 부르기뇽 : 프랑스에서 미식가의 유명한 지역 중 하나인 버건디식 요리를 말하며, 'Boeuf Bourguignonne'은 쇠고기를 주사위 모양으로 잘라서 작은 버섯과 양파와 함께 적포도주로 브레이징하는 요리이다.

á la Carte 알 라 카르트 : 각각의 음식마다 가격이 정해진 일품요리를 말한다.

á la King 알 라 킹 : 진한 크림 소스에 주사위 모양으로 자른 닭고기나 칠면조고기와 피망, 버섯을 첨가하여 만든 요리로서 셰리 와인을 넣기도 한다.

á la Mode 알 라 모드 : 프랑스에서는 '~풍의'를 의미하여 음식을 준비하는 스타일을 말하지만, 이 용어가 'Pie á la mode'와 같이 파이 위에 아이스크림을 얹어 먹는다는 의미로 미국화되었다.

al Dente 알 덴테 : 파스타나 식품을 삶을 때 부드럽거나 너무 익지 않게 삶아 약간 덜 익은 느낌의 씹히는 식감이 나게 삶은 것으로, 주로 파스타에 활용하지만 우리나라에서는 아직도 익숙하지 않은 조리법이다.

Alfredo Sauce 알프레도 소스 : 1920년대 로마에서 식당을 경영하던 알프레도(Alfredo di Lello)가 개발한 소스로서, 버터와 크림, 파마산 치즈, 검은 후추를 이용하여 진하게 만든 크림 소스이다.

Alla 알라 : '~와 함께, ~을 위하여' 등의 이탈리아어로서, 'Eggplant alla Parmigiana'는 가지 위에 토마토 소스, 모짜렐라, 파마산 치즈를 올려 만든 요리를 말한다.

Allemande Sauce 알르망드 소스 : 난황으로 농도를 되직하게 만든 벨루테로서 파리지엥 소스(Parisienne sauce)라고도 부른다.

Allumette 알루메트 : 성냥개비 모양과 크기로 자른 감자의 프랑스어로서 튀겨서 사용한다.

Anchovy 안초비 : 지중해와 남유럽 해안에서 잡히는 작은 은빛 생선인 안초비는 살을 발라서 소금에 절여 오일과 함께 통조림 한다. 통조림한 안초비는 상온에서 최소 1년 정도 저장할 수 있으며, 캔을 개봉한 안초비는 냉장고에 2개월 정도 보관할 수 있다. 안초비는 소스나 샐러드 드레싱이나 가니쉬로 사용한다.

Antipasta 안티파스토 : '식전'이란 의미를 가진 용어로 이탈리아에서는 차거나 뜨거운 오르되브르를 말하며, 치즈, 훈제고기, 올리브, 생선과 절인 채소 같은 애피타이저를 포함하고 있다.

Aperitif 아페리티프 : 점심 또는 저녁식사 전에 마시는 가벼운 알코올 음료로서 샴페인 (Champagne), 끼르(Kir), 쉐리(Cherry) 등의 식욕 촉진주를 말한다.

Appetizer 애피타이저 : 식전에 서비스되는 작은 한 입 크기의 음식으로서, 식욕을 촉진시키기 위해 테이블에 첫 코스로 제공하는 전채요리를 말한다.

Aromatic 아로마틱 : 싱싱한 향과 식음료의 맛을 전달하는 독특하고 감미로운 향을 지닌 허브와 스파이스(월계수 잎, 바질, 생강, 파슬리 등) 같은 여러 가지 식물을 뜻한다.

Aspic 아스픽 : 선명한 고기, 생선, 채소육수와 젤라틴으로 만든 투명한 향미의 젤리로서 아스픽은 잘게 혹은 사각으로 썰어서 찬 육류나 생선 등과 함께 렐리쉬로 사용한다.

au Jus 오 주 : 고기 자체의 육즙을 이용하여 만드는 것을 말하며, 일반적으로 쇠고기를 익힐 대 고유의 육즙을 이용하여 소스를 만들어야 맛이 좋다.

Bagurette 바게트 : 길고 좁은 원통형 모양의 프렌치 빵(french bread)으로서, 겉면은 밝은 갈색으로 바삭하고, 속은 쫄깃한 식감을 가지고 있으며, 프랑스의 대표적인 빵이다.

Bain Marie 뱅 마리 : 물을 담고 서서히 가열하여 음식이 타거나 식지 않도록 작은 용기에 담아 이중탕으로 일정한 온도가 유지되도록 사용하는 용기를 말하며, 주로 소스나 수프를 따뜻하게 보관하는 데 사용한다.

Bake 베이크 : 오븐의 공기대류현상과 복사열을 이용한 조리방법으로 170~240℃의 온도에서 굽는다. 조리속도는 느리지만 음식물의 표면에 접촉되는 건조한 열은 그 표면을 빠르게 구워 주어 그 맛을 높여 주며, 제과, 제빵 등에 많이 이용한다.

Baking Powder 베이킹파우더 : 밀가루 팽창제로서 액체와 결합하면 이산화탄소 가스를 발생시켜 반죽을 부풀게 한다.

Barbecue 바비큐 : 육류 및 가금류나 생선 등을 숯이나 장작을 이용한 직화열로 소스를 발라가며 서서히 굽는다. 지방이 빠지고 육즙이 잘 보존되어 담백하고 부드러운 맛과 숯불향이 일품이다.

Barding 바딩 : 지방을 얇게 썰거나 베이컨, 대망막 지방(caul fat) 등을 이용하여 기름기가 적은 재료에 싸서 굽는 동안 고기가 마르지 않고, 부드럽게 익으며, 고기즙을 풍부하게 만드는 데 도움을 준다. 고기가 익기 수 분 전에 갈색이 나도록 지방을 제거한다.

Baste 베이스트 : 오븐에서 조리하는 동안 고기의 표면이 마르지 않고 윤기 나며, 고기의 풍미를 증진시키기 위해 버터, 육즙, 육수 등을 고기 위에 끼얹어 주는 것을 뜻한다.

Baton, Batonnet 바톤, 바토네 : 프랑스어로 바게트보다 작은 빵조각을 의미하며, 채소나 페스트리 같은 작은 바톤 모양으로서, 일반적으로 성냥골 모양으로 썬 바톤과 바토네는 같은 의미로 사용한다.

Batter 배터 : 반죽이 흐르거나 스푼으로 뜰 수 있는 반 액체 형태로서 밀가루에 물이나 우유, 계란, 샐러드유 등을 섞은 반죽으로, 팬케이크, 와플, 머핀, 튀김옷 반죽 등으로 사용한다.

Bavarois 바바루아 : 커스터드, 휘핑크림, 여러 가지 과일이나 초콜릿, 럼주 등의 리큐르와 젤라틴을 섞어서 디저트로 만든 후 글라스잔이나 몰드에 담았다가 차게 식힌 후 스푼으로 떠먹는다.

Bearnaise 베어네즈 : 난황과 정제 버터를 섞은 다음 걸쭉해지면 식초, 와인, 타라곤, 샬롯을 넣어 졸인 액체를 첨가하여 부드럽게 만든 버터소스로서, 홀랜다이즈 소스와 같은 방법으로 만들며, 육류, 생선, 계란과 채소 요리와 함께 사용한다.

Beat 비트 : 원형으로 빠르게 젓는 행태로서 일반적으로 손으로 100회 젓는 것은 전동 믹서로 1분간 회전시키는 것과 같다. 생크림이나 계란 흰자는 저을 때 공기를 많이 주입시켜서 거품을 내야 음식이 완성되었을 때 훨씬 부드러운 식감을 낼 수 있다.

Béchamel 베샤멜 : 루이 14세 때 스튜워드 루이스 드 베샤멜이 개발한 기본인 모체 소스로서, 흰색 루(White roux)와 우유를 주재료로 만든 흰색 소스이다.

Beignet 베이네 : 기름에 튀긴 전통적인 뉴올리언즈 이스트 페스트리로서, 'Fritter'와 같은 튀김을 의미한다. 허브나 크랩은 매우 인기있는 튀김이다.

Beurre Blanc 뵈르 블랑 : 백포도주에 샬롯과 식초를 넣고 졸인 다음 버터로 몽테(monté)하여 만든 소스로서, 버터는 차고 단단한 버터를 사용한다. 가금류, 생선, 채소와 계란요리에 잘 어울린다.

Beurre Manié 뵈르 마니에 : 상온에 녹인 버터와 밀가루를 1:1로 섞어서 만든 페이스트인 농후제로 사용되며, 섞어 놓은 페이스트를 볶으면 루(roux)가 된다.

Beurre noir 뵈르 누아르 : 진한 갈색이 될 때까지 가열한 버터로 식초, 파슬리, 레몬주스, 허브, 케이퍼 등을 이용하여 계란, 생선, 채소요리에 사용한다.

Bisque 비스크 : 갑각류와 채소 및 토마토 페이스트를 볶아서 육수와 크림을 넣고 끓인 수프로서, 새우나 게 껍질 등을 많이 이용한다.

Blanch 블랜치 : 식품을 조리하거나 저장하기 전에 식품 고유의 색과 맛 및 형태를 유지하고, 냄새를 제거하기 위해 끓는 물에 살짝 데치거나 뜨거운 유지에 데치는 방법으로, 끓는 물에 데친 것은 더 이상 익지 않도록 찬 물이나 얼음물에 담갔다가 사용하거나 저장한다. 주로 나물류 무침이나 채소류 저장, 토마토 껍질 제거 등에 많이 활용하고 있다.

Blanquette 블랑케트 : 흰색 육수와 아로마틱 가니쉬를 넣고 송아지, 닭, 양 등을 양파, 양송이와 함께 익힌 후 육수에 흰색 루(roux)로 진하게 하고 리에종(크림+계란)으로 마지막 농도를 맞추어 희게 만든 스튜나 라구(ragout)이다.

Blini 블리니 : 블리니는 러시아에서 메밀가루를 이용하여 조그만 팬케이크처럼 만든 음식으로서, 사워 크림과 캐비아 또는 훈제 연어와 함께 먹는다.

Boiling 보일링 : 충분한 액체를 100℃ 이상의 끓는 물에서 익히는 방법으로 식재료를 연하게 해 주며, 감자, 건조채소, 뼈, 계란, 가금류 등을 익힐 때는 찬 물에 끓이고, 싱싱한 채소와 파스타류 등의 식품을 보다 빠르게 익히고, 비타민 및 기타 영양소와 식품 고유의 색을 보전할 때는 끓는 물에 넣고 삶는다.

Bouillabaise 부야베스 : 프로방스 지방의 생선 스튜로서, 생선부용에 어패류, 양파, 토마토, 와인, 올리브유, 마늘, 샤프랑, 허브를 넣고 향을 내서 바게트빵과 함께 제공한다.

Bouillon 부용 : 물에 가금류, 육류, 생선, 채소 등을 끓인 후 체에 걸러서 만든 육수로서, 수프와 소스의 기본이다.

Bouquet Garni 부케 가르니 : 여러 가지 향신료(월계수 잎, 파슬리, 타임, 양파, 정향, 통후추)를 실로 묶거나 천에 싸서 수프, 스튜, 소스의 향을 내기 위해 사용하는 향신료 꾸러미이다.

Braise 브레이즈 : 육류 또는 채소류를 기름에 갈색을 낸 후 적은 양의 액체를 넣은 다음 뚜껑을 닫고 낮은 온도로 천천히 조리하는 방법으로서, 천천히 조리하는 것은 맛을 향상시키고 섬유소를 파괴시켜 부드럽게 한다. 수분이 증발하지 못하도록 뚜껑을 완벽하게 닫아 주는 것이 중요하다.

Bread Crumbs 브레드 크럼 : 빵가루는 생산된지 하루 정도 지난 빵을 사용하는 것이 좋으며, 너무 부드럽거나 건조하지 않고 적당한 수분을 함유하고 있는 빵가루가 좋다.

Brisket 브리스켓 : 소 전체에서 앞쪽 1/4 부분의 배쪽 가슴살로서 1번에서 5번째 갈비 아래에 붙어있다. 고깃결이 있고 질기므로 오랫동안 익혀야 부드러워지며, 소금에 절여서 삶은 콘비프(corned beef)를 만들어 서양의 조식에 많이 사용한다.

Brochette 브로셰트 : 꼬챙이를 꽂아서 익힌 꼬치구이로서 'Skewer'를 말한다.

Broiling 브로일링 : 오븐이나 가스, 전기열 또는 숯불 등에 직화로 굽는 방법이다.

Broth 브로스 : 물이나 육수를 이용하여 육류나 채소를 넣어 만든 향미를 지닌 진한 액체를 말한다.

Brown Sauce 브라운 소스 : 기본적으로 갈색 육수와 갈색 루를 이용한 소스로서 현대에는 에스파뇰(espagnole sauce)이나 데미 글라스(demi-glace)와 같은 의미로 혼용하여 사용하며, 쇠뼈와 스지, 토마토 페이스트, 채소, 허브, 육수 등을 이용하고, 필요 시 갈색 루로 농도를 진하게 맞추어 사용한다.

Brunch 브런치 : 조식과 점심을 겸하여 먹는 식사로서 오전 11시에서 오후 3시 사이에 먹는다.

Brunoise 브뤼누아즈 : 정방형의 작은 주사위 모양으로 곱게 썬 채소로서, 수프나 소스 등에 사용한다.

Buffet 뷔페 : 식탁 위에 차려 놓은 다양한 요리를 고객 스스로 선택하여 직접 가져와 먹는 식사 방법이다.

Burgundy 버건디 : 프랑스 동부의 파리 최남단에 위치한 세계적으로 유명한 와인생산지역으로, 이 지역 와인을 이용한 요리가 많다.

Burrito 브리또 : 밀가루 토르티야(flour tortilla)를 이용하여 채를 썰거나 다진 고기, 콩, 체다 치즈, 사워 크림(sour cream), 양상추 등을 넣고 둥글게 말아서 만든 멕시코 요리를 말한다.

Butchery 부처리 : 육류, 가금류, 생선 등의 식품 재료를 조리하기 위해 도살 및 손질하여 요구하는 모양과 크기로 절단하고 가공하는 육가공 부서이다.

Butterfly 버터플라이 : 육류, 채소, 해산물 등을 한쪽 끝이 떨어지지 않도록 나비의 양 날개 모양처럼 반으로 잘라서 펼쳐 놓은 것으로서, 돼지 등심을 이용한 폭 커틀릿(pork cutlet)이나 새우 카나페 등을 만들 때 이용한다.

c

Cacao 카카오 : 열대 과일인 카카오나무의 열매(bean)로 코코아 버터, 초콜릿, 코코아 파우더를 만든다.

Cacciatora 카치아토라 : 헌터 스타일(hunter-style)로서 버섯, 양파, 토마토와 다양한 허브 그리고 와인을 이용하며, 치킨 카치아토라(chicken cacciatora)가 가장 인기 있는 요리이다.

Caesar Salad 시저 샐러드 : 1924년 멕시코 티주아나(Tijuana)에서 레스토랑을 운영하는 이탈리아 요리사 시저 카르디니(Caesar Cardini)에 의해 개발된 메뉴로서 전통적으로 마늘향의 식초 드레싱(garlic vinegar dressing), 파마산 치즈, 크루통(croton), 부드럽게 삶은 계란과 안초비(anchovies), 로메인 양상추를 섞어서 만든 샐러드를 말한다.

Cajun Seasoning 케이준 시즈닝 : 케이준 시즈닝은 다양한 레시피를 지니고 있지만, 일반적으로 마늘, 양파, 칠리, 검은 후추, 겨자와 셀러리를 포함하고 있다.

Calzone 칼조네 : 나폴리 지방의 피자로서, 여러 가지 고기류, 채소, 치즈 등의 스터핑(stuffing)을 피자도우에 올려 반으로 접어서 반달 모양으로 만든 피자로, 기름에 튀기거나 올리브유를 바르고 오븐에 굽는다.

Canapé 카나페 : 크래커나 작은 식빵 위에 계란, 치즈, 햄, 캐비아, 안초비 등을 얹어서 한

입에 들어갈 수 있게 만든 음식으로 애피타이저나 티파티 등에 사용한다.

Carbonara 카르보나라 : 크림, 계란, 치즈, 베이컨으로 구성된 파스타 소스로서, 파스타가 뜨거울 때 혼합물을 넣고 2~3분 정도 열을 가하면서 섞어 주어야 하나 계란이 너무 익어 덩어리가 생기지 않도록 하는 것이 중요하다.

Carte 카르트 : 메뉴(menu)라는 의미의 프랑스어이다.

Cassate 카사타 : 결혼식과 같은 축제일에 제공되는 이탈리아 디저트로서, 리코타 치즈, 과일 캔디, 얇은 스펀지 케이크와 초콜릿으로 층을 쌓아서 만든 것으로 차게 해서 먹으며, 스펀지 케이크 대신 아이스크림을 이용해서 만들기도 한다.

Casserole 캐서롤 : 뚜껑과 손잡이가 달린 움푹 들어간 그릇으로 오븐에 넣어 높은 열에서 견딜 수 있는 용기(유리, 철, 세라믹 등의 재질)로서, 육류, 채소, 밥, 콩 등을 이용하여 냄비에 요리하며, 치즈나 빵가루를 토핑으로 사용하기도 한다.

Cassoulet 카술레 : 프랑스의 랑귀덕(Languedoc) 지역의 요리로서, 다양한 육류(소시지, 돼지고기, 오리나 거위 콩피)와 토마토, 흰콩, 향신료 등을 끓여서 캐저롤에 담아 오븐에 넣고 그 위에 빵가루를 뿌려서 익힌 요리이다.

Caviar 캐비어 : 캐비아는 철갑상어알이 최상급으로서 종류로는 벨루가(beluga), 오세트라(osetra), 세브루가(sevruga)가 있으며, 이란과 러시아가 인접한 카스피 해에서 잡히는 벨루가 캐비아가 가장 좋은 품질이다. 철갑상어를 포획한 후 알을 채취하여 곧바로 가볍게 소금에 절여서 보관하였다가 고급 애피타이저나 카나페 등에 사용한다.

Celestine 셀레스틴 : 계란지단을 아주 작게 슬라이스한 조각으로서 콩소메(consomme) 수프에 가니쉬로 사용한다.

Chafing Dish 채핑 디시 : 뷔페 음식을 담아 따뜻하게 유지하기 위해서 사용하는 용기로서, 고체 알코올이나 전기장치를 이용하여 음식이 타거나 식지 않도록 중탕으로 가열한다.

Chanterelle 샹트렐 : 유럽에서 생산되는 샨터렐은 트럼펫 모양의 황갈색 버섯으로서, 씹는 질감과 너트맛 또는 과일맛을 지니고 있으며, 대부분 건조시키거나 통조림 형태로 유통되고 있다.

Charcuterie 샤퀴트리 : 15세기 이래 적어도 프랑스음식의 미적 기능과 관련된 샤퀴트리는 파테, 리에, 테린, 갈랑틴, 소시지 등의 돼지와 육류제품을 말한다.

Châteaubriand 샤토브리앙 : 19세기 프랑스작가인 프랑소와 샤토브리앙에 의해 붙여진 샤토브리앙은 사실상 소의 부위가 아니라 레시피로 쓰이고 있다. 쇠 안심의 중앙부분을 두툼하게 2인분으로 잘라서 사용되며, 고기를 그릴이나 브로일러에 구워서 베어네즈 소스와 샤또 감자 등을 곁들여 먹는다.

Chaud-Froid 쇼 프루와 : 프랑스어의 '뜨거운'과 '차가운'을 말하며, 육류, 가금류, 해산물을 익혀서 차갑게 식힌 후 아스픽(aspic)으로 윤기나게 처리하여 만든 음식을 말한다.

Cheese Cloth 치즈 크로스 : 수프와 소스를 만들 때 허브와 스파이스 꾸러미로 사용하거나 액체를 거를 때 사용하는 고운 그물망의 소창을 말한다.

Chiffon 시폰 : 공기를 주입으로 거품이 형성된 부드러운 반죽으로서, 파이 필링에 사용하며, 계란 흰자의 거품을 이용하여 만든다. 때때로 젤라틴을 이용하기도 한다.

Chiffonade 시폰나드 : 걸레를 만든다는 의미이지만, 요리측면으로는 채소를 가느다란 실과 같이 채를 썬 모양을 살짝 볶거나 생으로 장식 또는 수프 가니쉬 등에 많이 사용한다.

Chop 찹 : 육류를 칼이나 찹퍼(chopper)로 잘게 써는 방법으로, 푸드 프로세서로 갈 때는 거칠게 갈아서 사용한다.

Choucroute 슈크루트 : 사워크라우트(sauerkraut)의 프랑스어로서, 채 썬 양배추를 거위기름과 양파, 주니퍼베리, 카라웨이씨와 와인을 넣고 익히며, 소시지나 돼지고기, 햄, 거위 등의 육류를 감자와 함께 곁들인다.

Chowder 차우더 : 생선을 사각으로 잘라서 되직하게 만든 해산물 수프로서, 여러 가지 채소를 넣기도 한다.

Chutney 처트니 : 망고나 다른 과일류를 설탕, 식초, 향신료 등을 넣어 만드는 것으로 카레소스 등에 사용한다.

Ciseler 시즐레 : 요리시간을 줄이고 잘 익도록 생선 등에 칼집을 내는 것을 말한다.

Clarified Butter 정제 버터 : 버터의 유단백질과 수분을 제거하여 순수한 버터지방만 남아있게 정제한 버터로서, 버터를 끓이거나 중탕을 이용한다.

Cognac 코냑 : 프랑스의 코냑 지방에서 생산되는 백포도주를 원료로 하여 증류, 정제한 고급 브랜디로서, 스테이크를 구울 때 잡냄새를 제거하고 향을 돋우어 주며, 소스나 수프 등의 향미에도 사용한다.

Colander 콜랜더 : 구멍이 뚫린 둥근 볼로서 식품을 거르거나 물기를 제거하는 데 사용한다.

Cole Slaw 코울슬로 : 양배추를 곱게 썰어서 마요네즈를 섞어 만든 샐러드를 말한다.

Compote 콩포트 : 설탕시럽에 향과 리큐르를 첨가하여 과일을 먹기 좋은 크기로 잘라 넣고 익힌 것으로서, 배, 사과, 복숭아, 밀감 등을 이용하여 주로 조식 메뉴로 제공한다.

Compound Butter 콤파운드 버터 : 허브나 스파이스를 섞어서 만든 버터로서, 메트로호텔 버터, 안초비 버터, 허브 버터 등을 말하며, 그릴에 구운 스테이크나 채소류의 소스로 사용한다.

Condiment 콘디멘트 : 음식의 맛을 돋우어 주기 위한 재료로 겨자, 토마토케첩, 피클, 소스, 렐리쉬(relish) 등을 말한다.

Confit 콩피 : 허브, 소금 등으로 마리네이드한 후 오리나 거위 및 돼지기름으로 서서히 가열해서 만든 고기로서, 가끔씩 토마토, 피망 등을 이용한 콩피를 만들어서 음식의 가니쉬에 사용한다.

Consomme 콩소메 : 채소, 다진 고기, 계란 등을 넣고 끓여 국물을 맑게 한 수프로서, 쇠고기를 이용한 비프 콩소메, 닭고기를 사용한 치킨 콩소메, 토마토를 이용한 토마토 콩소메 등이 있다.

Coq au Vin 꼬꼬뱅 : 프랑스 중부지방의 요리로 적포도주와 야생닭, 버섯, 양파, 베이컨 또는 절인 돼지고기, 허브를 이용하여 만든 스튜요리이다.

Coral 코랄 : 바닷가재, 가리비 등과 같은 갑각류 알로서, 콤파운드 버터나 소스에 사용한다. 갑각류 알은 익히면 핑크빛으로 변하면서 아름다운 색깔의 소스를 만들 수 있다.

Cordon Bleu 코든 블루 : 프랑스어로 '파란색 리본'으로서 뛰어난 요리를 한 여자요리사에게 주어지는 상을 의미하였다. 요리의 의미로는 얇게 저민 송아지나 닭고기에 햄 또는 프로슈토(pros-ciutto)와 그뤼이어 치즈를 얇게 썰어 넣고 그 위에 또 다른 고기 조각을 덮어 빵가루를 입혀서 노릇하게 튀긴 음식을 말한다.

Coulis 쿨리 : 토마토 꿀리와 같이 진한 퓌레나 소스를 말하며, 진한 해산물 수프를 의미하기도 한다. 원래는 고기를 익힐 때 나오는 육즙을 표현한 것이다.

Court Bouillon 쿠르 부용 : 채소, 와인, 식초, 레몬주스, 허브 등으로 만든 육수로서 해산물과 채소를 포치하는 데 사용한다.

Couscous 쿠스쿠스 : 북아프리카 요리인 쿠스쿠스(전통적으로 couscousiere에 찜)는 기본적으로 양고기나 닭고기, 채소, 잠두콩(chickpeas), 건포도를 이용하여 만들며, 모르코는 사프란을, 알제리는 토마토를 추가하고, 튀니지는 매운맛의 하리사(harissa)라는 스파이스를 이용하여 맛을 낸다.

Crème Brûlée 크렘 브륄레 : 커스터드를 차게 식혀서 표면에 설탕을 뿌리고 맛을 내기 위해 빠르게 살라만더나 브로일러에 설탕을 캐러멜화해서 제공하는 디저트이다.

Crêpe 크레프 : 밀가루와 계란을 섞어 만든 반죽을 종이처럼 얇게 부친 팬케이크를 말하며, 설탕을 넣지 않은 플레인(plain) 반죽과 달콤한 디저트용 반죽을 만들어 고기, 치즈, 채소를 싸기도 하고, 사과, 잼, 꿀 등을 이용하여 디저트를 만들기도 한다. 대표적으로 오렌지 소스를 곁들이는 크렙 수제트가 있다.

Crépinette 크레피네트 : 다진 돼지고기, 양고기, 송아지고기나 닭고기, 송로버섯 등을 넣어 만든 작고 넓적한 소시지를 말하며, 크레핀(crépine)은 케이싱(casing)을 대신하여 크레피네(crépin-tte)를 싸는 돼지 대망막을 말한다.

Crespelle 크레스펠레 : 층 사이에 속재료를 넣거나 크렙(crêpe)처럼 둥글게 말거나 채워서 만드는 이탈리아 팬케이크

Crisp 크리스프 : 상추, 당근, 오이, 셀러리 등과 같은 채소를 얼음물에 담가서 단단하고 싱싱하게 된 것이거나 크래커나 바싹 구운 베이컨처럼 부서지기 쉬운 것을 의미한다.

Croque Monsieur 크로크 무슈 : 계란물에 담갔다가 그릴에 구운 프랑스식 햄과 치즈 샌드위치 또는 햄과 치즈를 넣은 샌드위치 빵을 컨베이어 오븐이나 샌드위치용 기계에 넣고 색이 나도록 구운 샌드위치를 말한다.

Croquette 크로켓 : 육류, 채소, 되직한 흰색 소스 등으로 반죽해서 원통형이나 타원형 또는 원형으로 만들어 밀가루, 계란물, 빵가루를 입혀서 튀긴 음식을 말한다.

Crostini 크로스티니 : 얇고 작게 썬 빵조각에 올리브유를 발라서 구운 토스트로, 이탈리아에서는 '작은 토스트'(lettle toast)라는 의미를 가지며, 카나페에 사용하기도 한다.

Crouton 크루톤 : 식빵을 사방 1~1.5cm 네모로 썰어 갈색으로 굽거나 튀긴 것으로, 수프나 샐러드 가니쉬로 사용한다.

Custard 커스터드 : 계란, 우유, 설탕의 혼합물에 소금과 향료를 적절히 넣어서 찜통에 찌거나 오븐에 구운 것으로 푸딩을 말한다.

Cutlet 커틀릿 : 소테나 그릴하기에 좋도록 얇고 작게 썬 고기조각이나 곱게 다진 고기나 생선, 계란 등을 넣어 커틀릿 모양으로 만든 것을 말하며, 계란물에 묻히고 빵가루를 입혀서 튀기기도 한다.

D

Dariole 다리올 : 작은 원통형의 몰드로서, 디저트를 구울 때 사용할 뿐만 아니라 아몬드 크

림과 같이 속재료를 퍼프 도우(puff dough)를 붙인 몰드에 넣어 오븐에 굽거나 채소 커스터드를 만든다.

Deglaze 디글레이즈 : 고기를 익힌 후 과잉기름을 버리고 육수나 와인을 넣고 졸여서 즙으로 만드는 것으로, 소스의 기본재료로 사용한다.

Demi Glace 데미 글라스 : 육수를 마데라 와인이나 셰리 와인을 함께 넣고 절반(Half)으로 줄 때까지 서서히 끓여서 진하게 만들어 다양한 소스를 만드는 기본 소스로 사용한다. 실무에서는 토마토 페이스트를 넣고 색깔을 내어 갈색 소스의 기본으로 사용한다.

Dice 다이스 : 식품재료를 1/8~1/4인치 크기의 주사위 모양으로 써는 것을 말하며, 스튜요리할 때 고기나 채소를 썰거나 한입 크기의 가니쉬로 장식 시 사용한다.

Dough 도우 : 액체와 발효제 등의 다른 재료를 밀가루와 함께 섞어서 너무 묽거나 되직하지 않게 하여 손으로 취급가능할 수 있도록 만든 반죽으로, 라비올리, 피자반죽 등과 같은 반죽을 말한다.

Dredge 드레즈 : 음식을 굽기 전에 밀가루, 옥수수가루, 빵가루 등을 굴리거나 음식 위에 뿌려서 식품에 옷을 입히는 것을 말한다.

Dumpling 덤플링 : 밀가루, 빵가루, 치즈, 고기 등을 이용해 경단 모양으로 만들어 찌거나 삶아서 수프나 요리로 이용한다.

Durum Wheat 드럼 밀 : 파스타에 사용하는 세몰리나를 만들기 위해서 사용하는 단단한 밀의 일종으로서 우리나라 국수처럼 스파게티가 쉽게 퍼지지 않고 단단한 이유이다.

Duxelle 뒥셀 : 곱게 다진 샬롯과 버섯, 향신료를 첨가하여 버터로 서서히 볶아 만든 재료로서, 소스나 수프뿐만 아니라 비프 웰링턴과 같은 음식을 만드는 재료로 사용한다.

e

Emince 에멩세 : 재료를 가늘고 얇게 저며 써는 것으로, 고기의 결이 촘촘히 잘려 고기의 질감을 좀 더 부드럽게 하는 데 도움이 된다.

Escalope 에스칼로프 : 육류나 생선을 얇고 넓적하게 썬 고기조각으로, 고기를 구울 때 짧은 시간 내에 익혀서 부드러운 맛을 내며, 영어로는 Scallop이라고 한다.

Essence 에센스 : 생선, 민트, 채소나 꽃과 같은 식재료에서 얻은 추출물이나 바닐라 에센스와 같이 어떤 물질로부터 추출된 농축의 추출물을 말한다.

F

Fillet 필레 : 뼈를 발라낸 생선이나 가금류의 살로서 쇠고기 안심을 Beef Fillet이라고도 한다.

Flambé 플람베 : 음식에 알코올을 부려 불꽃을 내며 그을리는 것으로, 냄새제거와 향을 내며, 손님에게도 시각적인 효과를 낸다.

Flavor 플레이버 : 음식의 맛, 풍미, 향미 등을 말하며, 요리에서 가장 중요한 요소이기도 한다.

Fleuron 플뢰롱 : 퍼프도우(puff dough)를 모형 틀로 찍어 반달 모양을 만들어 구운 것으로, 수프나 생선 등에 곁들여 준다.

Florentine A la 플로랑틴 알 라 : '프로방스 지방 스타일로'라는 의미로서 주로 시금치를 깔고 계란이나 생선을 올리고 모르네 소스를 부려서 만든다.

Food mill 푸드 밀 : 삶은 채소나 감자를 퓌레로 만들거나 가는 기구로서 으깬 감자(mashed potato)를 만들 때 사용한다.

Forcemeat 포스미트 : 육류나 생선을 곱게 다지거나 갈아서 다른 재료를 혼합한 것으로, 파테, 테린, 소시지 등을 만들 때 사용한다.

Fricassee 프리카세 : 채소와 함께 스튜를 하기 전에 버터를 이용하여 주로 닭고기를 볶는 것을 말하며, 와인향의 두툼한 고기의 스튜를 만든다.

Fritter 프리터 : 반죽을 입혀서 튀긴 음식으로 베네(beignet)라고도 하며, 사과, 옥수수, 게살 등을 튀긴다.

Fritto Misto 프리토 미스토 : 여러 종류의 먹기 좋은 크기의 채소나 육류, 생선을 반죽(batter)에 묻힌 튀김이다.

Fumet 퓌메 : 생선, 버섯 등의 향미식품을 액체와 와인에 음식을 익힘으로써 우러나온 맛이 진한 육수이다.

G

Game 게임 : 사슴, 곰, 산토끼, 버팔로 소 등과 같은 식용의 야생동물을 말한다.

Garnish 가니쉬 : 음식 위를 장식하거나 고기와 함께 먹을 수 있고 보기 좋게 장식하기 위해서 곁들이는 채소와 부재료를 말한다.

Gelatin 젤라틴 : 냄새와 맛 및 색깔이 없는 농후제로서 뜨거운 물에 녹고, 차가우면 젤리형태를 이룬다. 젤라틴은 쇠뼈, 연골 등에서 추출된 순수 단백질이며, 요즈음에는 돼지 껍질에서도 가공한다. 테린이나 찬 요리를 되직하게 농도를 맞추는 등의 용도에 사용한다. 기공한 단백질은 40·50℃ 물에 용해된다.

Ghee 기 : 물소의 젖으로 만드는 기는 인도가 원산지이지만, 요즈음은 네덜란드, 스칸디나비아, 호주 등지에서 생산하고 있으며, 산양과 소의 젖으로도 만든다. 기는 발연점이 375℉ 정도로 일반 정제 버터보다 높아 재료를 볶고 튀기는 데 실용적이다.

Gherkin 게르킨 : 작은 청오이는 피클을 만들기 위해 특별히 경작하며, 절여서 항상 병에 담아 판매되는 거어킨은 소스나 렐리쉬(relish) 등으로 사용한다.

Giblets 지블레 : 가금류의 간, 심장, 목 등을 말하며, 오리나 거위 부산물을 이용하여 만든 지블렛 소스가 맛이 좋다.

Glace de Viande 글라스 드 비앙드 : 쇠뼈를 야채와 함께 오랫동안 고아서 농축시킨 미트 글레이즈(meat glaze)로서, 농축된 육수를 계란 흰자와 채소를 이용하여 정제시킨 맑고 진한 갈색 소스를 말한다.

Glaze 글레이즈 : 음식에 윤기나게 소스를 바르거나 페스트리 표면에 계란을 발라 오븐에서 노릇노릇하고 윤기있게 구워내는 것을 말한다.

Goujonette 구조네트 : 누들 파스타 모양으로 자른 생선을 보기 좋게 새끼를 꼬거나 서로 엮어서 요리한다.

Grand Marnier 그랑 마니에르 : 리큐르 술로서 오렌지향이 나는 품질 좋은 꼬냑으로 디저트 소스를 만드는 데 사용한다.

Gravlax 그라블랙스 : 스칸디나비아 음식으로 싱싱한 연어 필레를 소금, 설탕, 딜(dill)을 이용해 마리네이드하여 전채요리나 샌드위치에 이용하고, 딜향의 겨자 소스와 함께 곁들여 먹으면 좋다.

Guacamole 과카몰레 : 아보카도 퓌레에 레몬주스와 홍고추, 칠리파우더 같은 양념을 넣거나 추가적으로 다진 양파, 실파, 고수를 섞어 만든 소스로 다양한 멕시코 음식에 곁들인다.

H

HACCP : Hazard Analysis Critical Control Point의 약자로 식품의 안전성을 확보하기 위해서 취급하는 식품을 단계별로 모니터하는 시스템이다. 안전한 식품 취급 방법뿐만 아니라 관리법이 시간과 온도에 따라 확립되어 있다.

Hashed Brown Patatoes 해쉬드 브라운 포테이토 : 감자를 살짝 삶아 잘게 채친 후 다진 양파 및 베이컨과 함께 갈색으로 볶아서 조식 계란요리와 함께 곁들여 먹는다.

Hollandaise 홀랜다이즈 : 모체 소스 중의 하나로 정제 버터, 난황, 식초, 레몬주스 등을 이용하여 마요네즈처럼 만들지만, 소스 보관은 마요네즈와 반대로 따뜻하게 보관한다.

Hors d'Oeuvre 오르되브르 : 아페리티프나 칵테일과 함께 식전에 제공하는 애피타이저로서, 차거나 따뜻한 작은 크기의 음식

Hotel Pan 호텔팬 : 뷔페음식이나 식품의 저장 등에 사용하는 직사각형의 금속팬으로 여러 가지 표준크기가 있다.

i

Inventory 인벤토리 : 월말 또는 월초를 기준으로 현재 보유하고 있는 상품의 종류와 수량을 파악하여 영업장의 원가관리의 기초자료로 사용한다.

J

Julienne 쥘리엔느 : 성냥개비 형태의 1/8인치 두께로 일정하게 채를 썬 음식으로, 수프, 가니쉬 등에 많이 사용한다.

K

Kabab 케밥 : 마리네이트(marinate)한 고기와 생선조각을 꼬챙이에 끼워 숯불에 굽는 음식으로, 채소를 함께 끼워 사용하기도 한다.

Kosher 코셔 : 먹을 수 있는 음식의 형태뿐만 아니라 하나의 식사에 섞을 수 있는 음식의 종류도 엄격한 유대교의 율법에 따라 준수하여야 하는데, 이러한 음식을 "Kosher Foods"라고 한다.

Kosher Salt 코셔 소금 : 순수하게 정제한 소금으로, 코셔 음식을 만들 때나 피클을 만들 때 사용한다.

L

Lard 라드 : 조리 시 즙을 풍부하게 하거나 고기의 질감을 부드럽게 하기 위해 고기 속에 끼워 넣는 지방이나 베이컨의 작은 조각을 말한다.

Liaison 리에종 : 수프, 소스 등의 액체를 진하게 하는 것으로 븨흐 마니에(beurre manie), 루(roux), 난황 또는 농도를 진하게 만드는 성분 중에 밀가루, 옥수수전분, 갈분과 같은 물질을 이용하여 농도를 맞춘다.

Lyonnaise 리오네즈 : 리용 지방의 음식으로, 양파를 넣어 만드는 요리로서 리용식 감자요리나 리오네즈 소스 등이 있다.

M

Macaroni 마카로니 : 강력분으로 만든 구멍이 뚫린 관 모양의 파스타로서 마카로니 그라틴이나 샐러드 등에 사용한다.

Madeira 마데이라 : 포르투갈령의 대서양 군도의 이름으로서 마데이라섬에서 생산한 적포도주이다.

Mandoline 만돌린 : 스테인리스 스틸로 만든 채칼로서 감자칩, 와플 감자, 채썰기 등을 할 수 있는 칼날을 조절할 수 있다.

Marinate 마리네이트 : 고기를 연하고 향을 좋게 하기 위하여 향신료나 식초, 기름 등에 재료를 재워 두는 것을 말한다.

Marmite 마마이트 : 카졸레와 같이 오랫동안 요리할 수 있도록 뚜껑이 달린 옆면이 평평하고 깊은 요리냄비이다.

Marsala 마르살라 : 시실리섬의 마스랄라 지방 인근지역에서 재배되는 포도로 제조, 생산한 semi-dry 와인이다.

Marzipan 마지팬 : 아몬드, 설탕, 계란 흰자로 만든 아몬드 페이스트로, 페스트리 속을 넣거나 장식하는 데 사용한다.

Medallion 메달리온 : 주로 쇠고기, 송아지 또는 돼지고기의 작은 동전 모양의 고기조각을 말한다.

Mel ba Toast 멜바 토스트 : 쉐프인 아우구스트 에스코피에가 오페라가수인 넬리 멜바를 위해 개발한 얇게 썰어 토스트한 식빵조각으로 수프나 샐러드 등에 사용한다.

Meringue 머랭 : 거품을 낸 계란 흰자에 설탕을 섞어 놓은 반죽으로 구워서 사용한다.

Milanaise á la 밀라네즈 알 라 : 프랑스 조리용어로서 햄, 절인 소 혀, 양송이버섯, 송로버섯을 넣은 토마토 소스에 치즈를 섞어 만든 파스타를 말한다.

Milanese alla 밀라네제 알라 : '밀라노식으로'란 이탈리아어로서 재료를 계란물에 적시고 빵가루와 파마산 치즈가루를 섞은 혼합물을 묻혀 전을 만들 듯이 팬에 버터를 둘러서 지진 음식이다.

Mille-feuille 밀푀유 : 프랑스어로 '천 개의 잎'이란 뜻으로서 바삭한 퍼프 페이스트리(puff pastry) 한장에 거품낸 크림, 커스터드, 잼, 또는 과일 퓌레를 펼치고, 또 다른 페스트리를 위해 덮은 다음 크기에 따라 잘라서 디저트로 사용하거나, 치즈를 채워서 애피타이저로 제공할 수 있다.

Mince 민스 : 식품을 아주 작은 조각으로 다진 것으로, 햄버거 패티(patty)나 완자 등을 만들 때 사용한다.

Mirepoix 미르포아 : 여러 가지 육수, 소스 등에 넣는 잘게 썬 채소로써 음식의 풍미를 증진시키며, 일반적으로 양파, 당근, 셀러리를 5:3:2의 비율로 사용한다.

Mise en Place 미즈 앙 플라스 : '적절한 자리에 놓다'라는 의미로, 음식을 만들기 위해 필요한 재료, 조리도구, 접시 등을 미리 준비하여 정해진 장소에 정리하는 것을 말한다.

Misto 미스토 : 이탈리아어로 '섞다'라는 의미로서, 예를 들면 프리또 미스토(frito misto)는 모듬튀김을 뜻하는 것이다.

Mold 몰드 : 빵, 테린, 파테 등을 만들기 위해 오븐에 굽기 위한 형틀

Monté 몽테 : '휘젓는다'는 뜻으로 딱딱한 버터를 뜨거운 소스에 넣고 휘저으면서 녹여 풍부한 맛과 농도를 걸쭉하게 만든다.

Mousse 무스 : 크림, 계란, 젤라틴, 초콜릿, 과일 등과 같은 향미제를 사용하여 만든 부드럽고 맛있는 디저트이다.

Mousseline 무슬린 : 소스에 거품을 낸 크림이나 계란 흰자를 추가하거나, 흰 살코기나 생선을 곱게 갈아서 크림이나 계란 흰자를 넣어 부드럽게 만든 음식을 말한다.

N

Noisette 누아제트 : 헤이즐넛 또는 작은 갈비살 덩어리를 말한다.

O

Oblique Cut/Roll Cut 오블리크 컷 : 원통형의 채소를 사선으로 반을 자른 다음 180도 돌려서 같은 사선으로 썰어서 두 개의 각진 가장자리를 갖는 모형썰기를 말한다.

Omelet 오믈렛 : 오믈렛 팬에 버터나 식용유를 두르고 풀어 놓은 계란을 넣어 휘저으면서 속은 부드럽고 수분이 생기지 않게 타원형의 오믈렛을 만들며, 계란에 넣는 속재료는 필요에 따라 달리한다.

Onion Pique 어니언 피케 : 정향을 월계수 잎과 함께 꽂은 양파로서 베샤멜 소스나 수프의 향미를 내는 데 사용한다.

P

Paella 파에야 : 닭고기, 홍합, 토마토, 양파, 피망, 초리죠(chorizo) 소시지 등을 넣고 사프란을 첨가하여 만든 대표적인 스페인 밥요리이다.

Panada 빠나다 : 밀가루나 빵가루를 우유나 육수에 익혀서 반죽한 것으로 간 생선이나 육류의 결착제로 사용한다.

Papillote 파피요트 : 내용물을 찜통에 찌기 전에 호일이나 유산지·시금치·양배추 잎 등으로 싸서 찌는 방식으로, 가니쉬는 내용물과 함께 쪄서 사용한다.

Parfait 파르페 : 아이스크림과 과일이나 여러 가지 맛을 지닌 시럽을 여러 층이 형성되도록 만든 냉동 디저트이다.

Paupiette 포피에트 : 가자미와 같은 얇은 생선을 코르크 모양으로 동그랗게 마는 것으로, 스터핑(stuffing)을 넣어서 만들기도 하고, 연어와 같은 생선을 포떠서 만들기도 하며, 베이컨을 말기도 한다. 포피에트는 룰라드(roulade)라고 부르기도 한다.

Pesto 페스토 : 바질과 호두·잣·올리브유·치즈 등을 넣고 믹서에 갈아서 걸쭉하게 만든 퓨레로 파스타나 생선 소스에 사용한다.

Petit Four 프티 푸르 : 한입 크기로 당의를 입혀서 만든 작은 케이크이다.

Pilaf 필라프 : 쌀을 버터에 살짝 볶은 다음 향신료와 육수를 넣고 서서히 수분이 없도록 익히는 요리로서, 다져서 익힌 채소·육류·생선 등을 함께 넣을 수도 있다.

Polenta 폴렌타 : 거친 옥수수가루로 만든 폴렌타는 버터와 함께 뜨겁게 먹을 수도 있고, 식혀서 먹기도 한다. 폴렌타는 때때로 치즈와 섞어 먹기도 한다.

Potato Chip 포테이토 칩 : 19세기 중엽 뉴욕에 있는 사라토가 스프링스호텔의 요리사가 개발한 얇게 썰어서 튀긴 과자로서 사라토가 칩(saratoga chips)이라고도 부른다.

Pot au Feu 포토피 : 가금류나 쇠고기를 부드럽게 삶아서 뿌리채소와 함께 브로스(broth)에 담아내는 요리로, 육수를 먼저 제공하고, 고기와 채소를 뒤따라 내놓기도 한다.

Profiterolle 프로피트롤 : 계란과 소금 등을 섞어 만든 반죽을 부풀게 튀겨서 만든 작은 퍼프 페스트리로서 속에 크림·치즈 등을 채워서 사용한다.

Provencal 프로방샬 : 프랑스 프로방스 지방의 음식으로 마늘·토마토·올리브유를 사용하고, 안초비·가지·버섯·양파·올리브가 들어가기도 한다.

Q

Quenelle 퀜넬 : 육류나 해산물을 이용하여 포스미트를 만들어 계란을 섞은 다음 끓는 물에 새알크기와 모양을 만들어 익힌 완자로서 수프 등에 사용한다.

R

Raclette 라클렛 : 유명한 스위스 치즈로, 치즈를 녹여 삶은 감자와 거킨(gherkin)을 곁들여 먹는다.

Ratatouille 라타투이 : 가지, 토마토, 양파, 피망, 주키니, 마늘, 허브를 올리브유에 익힌 프랑스 프로방스 지역의 채소 요리로서 양고기 등의 가니쉬로 사용한다.

Rillette 리예트 : 기름에 서서히 익혀 잘게 다진 돼지고기나 오리고기 또는 거위고기를 양념하고 기름에 섞어서 만든 혼합물로 메밀 빵(rye bread) 등과 함께 먹는다.

Risotto 리소토 : 버터에 쌀을 살짝 볶은 다음 육수를 조금씩 반복적으로 넣고 저으면서 약간 덜 익힌 알단테(al dente)가 될 때가지 끓여 주는 쌀요리로서 레시피에 따라 해산물·버섯·허브 등을 넣는다.

Roux 루 : 수프나 소스의 기초가 되는 것으로서 밀가루와 버터를 동량으로 넣고 볶은 것이고, 흰색 루, 브론드 루, 갈색 루를 만들어 사용한다.

S

Sabayon 사바용 : 계란·설탕·백포도주 등을 넣고 중탕으로 만든 소스이다.

Sago 사고 : 야자수 나무에서 얻어지는 밀가루 같은 물질로, 농후제나 디저트로 사용한다.

Sauté 소테 : 프라이팬에 소량의 기름으로 센 불에 빨리 볶는 것으로, 가장 많이 사용하는 조리법 중의 하나이다.

Searing 시어링 : 로스트·브레이즈·스튜 등을 하기 위해 뜨거운 프라이팬이나 브로일러 또는 오븐을 이용하여 강한 불에서 빠른 시간 내에 음식의 겉만 갈색이 나게 지지는 것으로, 육즙이 밖으로 나오지 못하도록 하는 데 목적이 있다.

Sheet Pan 시트 팬 : 얇고 평평한 사각팬으로 다양한 음식이나 빵을 오븐에 구울 때 사용한다.

Sift 시프트 : 가루로 된 식품 재료를 체에 쳐서 덩어리가 없어지도록 거르는 것을 말한다.

Simmer 시머 : 액체 등이 끓지 않도록 약한 불로 서서히 조리하는 것으로, 생선 등을 부드럽게 익히는 조리법이다.

Skim 스킴 : 음식을 조리하는 동안 육수나 수프와 같은 액체의 표면에 뜬 기름이나 이물질·불순물을 제거하여 잡내를 없애면서 육수를 맑게 한다.

Smoking 스모킹 : 식품을 여러 가지 향미를 주면서 연기로 익히는 훈제방법으로, 저온훈제법과 고온훈제법이 있다.

Sorbet 셔벗 : 여러 가지 과일주스를 이용하여 설탕과 난백을 섞어 만든 디저트로, 계란 흰자는 얼음의 결정을 세밀하게 만들어 준다.

soufflé 수플레 : '부풀린'이란 뜻으로, 밀가루·계란·우유 등으로 반죽하여 부풀게 만든 요리나 디저트이고, 포테이토 수플레나 바닐라 수플레 등이 있다.

Spaetzle 스패츨 : 독일음식으로 계란·우유·물 등을 넣은 밀가루반죽이 부드러워지도록 치대어 콜렌더나 동그란 구멍이 뚫린 체를 통과시켜 끓는 물에 떨어뜨리면 짧은 국수나 작은 수제비 형태의 덤플링이 만들어진다.

Steep 스티프 : 차·커피·허브 등을 뜨거운 물에 담가서 색과 맛이 우러나게 하는 것을 말한다.

Stew 스튜 : 질긴 고기를 이용하여 국물을 붓고 저온으로 장시간 끓여 부드럽게 만드는 요리로서 비프 스튜가 대표적이다.

Stir Frying 스터 프라잉 : 중국 프라이팬(wok)을 이용하여 강한 불에 소량의 기름을 두르고 재료를 넣은 다음 흔들어 주면서 볶는다.

Stock 스톡 : 수프·소스 등을 만들기 위하여 육류·채소 등을 끓인 국물로서, 이때 사용하는 커다란 냄비를 스톡 포트(stock pot)라고 한다.

Stuffing 스터핑 : 속을 채우는 것으로서 계란·오이·토마토·닭·생선 등의 음식에 다른 식품을 채워 넣어 요리하는 것을 말한다.

Syrup 시럽 : 끓는 물에 설탕을 녹여 만든 것을 설탕시럽(sugar syrup)이라 하며, 귤껍질과 같은 향미물질을 첨가하기도 한다.

Table d'Hôte 타블 도트 : 주요리 선택에 따라 가격이 정해져 있는 코스요리를 말한다.

Tart 타트 : 전채나 디저트를 위한 도우를 밀어서 오븐에 구운 동그란 페스트리 크러스트(pastry crust)에 음식이나 달콤한 재료를 얹어 사용하며, 한입 크기의 작은 타트를 타틀렛(tartlet)이라고 한다.

Terrine 테린 : 육류나 생선 등을 곱게 갈아 몰드에 넣고 중탕으로 익히는 것으로 식혀서 6~7mm 정도 크기로 썰어 사용한다.

Timbale 팀벨 : 곱게 간 고기에 양념을 하고 야채와 계란을 첨가하여 조그만 원통형 틀에 넣고 이중탕으로 익힌 음식이나 형틀을 말한다.

Tripe 트라이프 : 소와 같은 반추동물의 식용 가능한 위의 내벽으로, 벌집위는 두 번째 위의 내벽이다.

Truffle 트러플 : 프랑스·이탈리아 등지에서 수퇘지에 의해 채취되는 호두 모양 같은 흰색과 검은색 등의 송로버섯으로, 소스·파테 등의 다양한 요리에 이용된다.

Vanilla Sauce 바닐라 소스 : 우유나 크림 또는 설탕·계란을 중탕하여 바닐라향으로 맛을 낸 소스를 말한다.

Velouté 벨루테 : 모체 소스 중의 한 가지로 브론드 루와 육수(닭육수·송아지육수·생선육수)를 사용하여 만든 소스로서 수프나 흰색 소스의 기본이다.

Vermicelli 버미첼리 : 수프·샐러드·볶음 등에 사용되는 길고 아주 가느다란 파스타의 일종이다.

Vichy 비시 : 보통 당근을 비행접시 모형으로 깎는 것으로, 프랑스 비시 지방에서 비롯되었다.

Vichyssoise 비시스와즈 : 감자, 닭육수, 크림 등을 이용한 찬 감자 수프로 다진 차이브(chive)를 곁들인다.

Vinaigrette 비네그레트 : 일반적으로 오일과 식초를 3:1의 비율로 배합한 드레싱으로, 여러 가지 향신료를 첨가한다.

Vol au Vent 볼로방 : 퍼프 도우(puff dough)를 이용하여 다양한 모양으로 구운 페스트리로서 흰색 소스를 곁들인 생선·육류 등의 요리를 채워 넣는다.

w

Waffle 와플 : 철판과 뚜껑을 격자로 만든 와플기계를 이용하여 버터·밀가루·우유, 계란 등의 반죽(batter)으로 바삭하게 구운 것으로, 단풍당시럽(maple syrup)과 버터를 곁들여 조식으로 먹는다.

Whip 휩 : 계란 흰자, 크림 등과 같은 재료를 공기와 함께 휘저어서 거품을 내는 것으로, 반죽을 부풀게 하고 음식을 부드럽게 해 주는 역할을 한다.

Wok 웍 : 바닥이 둥글고 움푹 패인 중국음식용 팬으로서 중국요리에서 음식을 볶을 때 사용한다.

y

Yam 얌 : 열대와 아열대 지방에서 잘 자라는 줄기식물로서 과육에 전분이 많다.

Yolk 요크 : 계란 노른자(난황)로서 페스트리 표면의 색이 잘 나도록 바르고 굽거나 홀랜다이즈 소스를 만들 때 등 다양하게 사용한다.

참고문헌 및 참고사이트

강경재(2013). Guide to the Culinary Industry. 백산출판사.

김상철 외(2015). 호텔조리실무영어. 지구문화사.

김귀원(2013). Hotel Service English. 백산출판사.

이수부, 김태현, 김태형(2014). 조리영어. 교문사.

김태현(2017). 한식조리사를 위한 키친잉글리시. 교문사.

한선희(2017). 나는 레스토랑영어다. 기문사.

Milada Broukal(1994). Weaving It Together. Heinle & Heinle.

Rob Jordens & Terry Jordens(2009). Talk about Travel. Compass Publishing.

Steven J. Molinsky & Bill Bliss(1998). SBS TV Video Coursebook. Prentice Hall Regents.

Tina Kasloff Carver & Sandra Douglas Fortinos(1998). A Conversation Book 1A. Prentice Hall Regents.

https://en.islcollective.com

https://www.scribd.com

https://busyteacher.org

https://www.easypacelearning.com

http://culinary.utk.edu

https://www.easypacelearning.com

저자
소개

한선희 교수는 경북여고 및 경북대학교 사범대학 영어교육과와 동 대학원을 졸업하고 경희대학교에서 문학박사(영어학)를 취득하였다. 현재 대림대학교 호텔외식서비스과 교수로 재직하면서 레스토랑영어, 키친잉글리시, 호텔서비스엉어 능늘 강의하고 있다.

저서 및 논문
- Prosody in Lexical Phonology: Cases in English and Korean (박사학위논문)
- 한국어의 운율구조
- 한국어 운율경계의 음성–음향적 특질 연구
- 대화체 억양구말 형태소의 경계성조 연구
- Writing Start
- Becoming Writers
- Traveler's English
- English for Cabin Crew
- 하늘을 나는 영어
- 나는 레스토랑영어다 등 다수

박미선 교수는 고려대학교 영어영문학과와 미국 델라웨어대학교 언어학과 대학원을 졸업하고, 미국 컬럼비아대학교 교육대학원에서 TESOL 전공으로 교육학석사와 교육학박사를 취득하였으며, 미국 컬럼비아대학교에서 학술적 글쓰기와 말하기(academic writing and speaking)를 강의하였다.

저서 및 논문
- An exploratory study of foreign accent and phonological awareness in Korean learners of English (박사학위논문)
- Orthographic Input and the Acquisition of Second Language Phonology : A Review
- Effects of Explicit Pronunciation Instruction on the Development of Second Language Syllable Structure 등 다수

저자와의
합의하에
인지첩부
생략

I'm Kitchen English(나는 키친 잉글리시다)

2018년 8월 25일 초 판 1쇄 발행
2019년 7월 30일 개정판 1쇄 발행

지은이 한선희 · 박미선
펴낸이 진욱상
펴낸곳 (주)백산출판사
교 정 편집부
본문디자인 박채린
표지디자인 오정은

등 록 2017년 5월 29일 제406-2017-000058호
주 소 경기도 파주시 회동길 370(백산빌딩 3층)
전 화 02-914-1621(代)
팩 스 031-955-9911
이메일 edit@ibaeksan.kr
홈페이지 www.ibaeksan.kr

ISBN 979-11-89740-63-4 13740
값 18,000원